FOOTPRINTS ACROSS OUR LAND

FOOTPRINTS ACROSS OUR LAND

short stories by senior Western Desert women

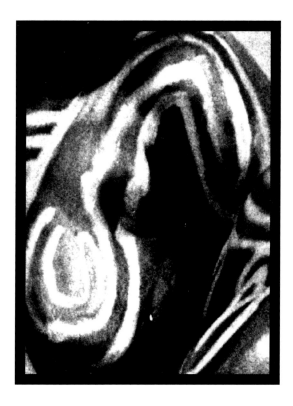

LUMU NUNGURRAYI • MARRI YAKUNY NAPURRULA • MILYIKA NAPALTJARRI • NANCY KUNGKULU TAX • NINGI NANGALA • NGUNYTJA NAPANANGKA MOSQUITO • NYANGAYI NAPANGARTI • TJAMA NAPANANGKA • KUNINYI NAMPITJIN • YUKA NAPANANGKA • YUNITJA NAMPITJIN • YUPINYA NAMPITJIN • YUTJUYU TAAMPA NAMPITJIN

Compiled by Jordan Crugnale

MAGABALA BOOKs

First published by Magabala Books Aboriginal Corporation
Broome Western Australia 1995

Magabala Books receives financial assistance from the State Government of Western
Australia through the Department for the Arts; the Aboriginal and Torres Strait Islander
Commission; and the Aboriginal and Torres Strait Islander Arts Board of the Australia
Council, the Federal Government's arts funding and advisory body.

Designer Samantha Cook
Editor Peter Bibby, Rachel Bin Salleh
Production Co-ordinator Grant Drage
Colour Separations by CDC Graphics
Printed by Lamb Printers Pty Ltd
Typeset in New Baskerville 12/14

National Library of Australia
Cataloguing-in-Publication data

Footprints across our land.

ISBN 1 875641 15 7.

[1.] Kukatja (Australian people) – Social life and customs.
[2.] Kukatja (Australian people) – Women. I. Nungurrayi, Lumu II. Crugnale, Jordan.

305.48899150941

Acknowledgements

We would like to thank the Wirrimanu, Malarn and Yaka Yaka communities; Michelle Mackenzie for her overwhelming support and dedication to the Manungka Manungka Women's Association and this project; Anna Mardling from the Kimberley Language Resource Centre, Halls Creek; Vonnie Brown, Mindy Oxenburg, Gabrielle Verstraete, Peter Bibby, Judith Ryan, Leah Grycewicz, Patrick Moffatt, Peter Thompson and Judyth Watson.

Thanks also to the Australia Council for their financial assistance.

Paintings by the storytellers
Photographs by Jordan Crugnale

Preface

The following collection of short stories was told by a group of senior Kukatja, Wangkajunga and Ngarti women based at Wirrimanu and Yaka Yaka communities. The women present their perspective on living in the desert, Tjukurrpa (Dreaming) and their encounters with kartiya (white people) in the 1930s and 1940s.

The project was initiated by the women themselves who were concerned that their stories, knowledge and history would disappear with nothing written down for the future generations of their community.

The project began in 1992 as part of the bi-lingual program in Wirrimanu, where Kukatja is the lingua franca. It was intended to compile and publish a bi-lingual book for the secondary girls. All stories were recorded on tape and then translated into Aboriginal English over an eight-month period. Most of the storytelling and paintings were done on a trip away from the community to sites nominated by the women. This allowed them to visit their country, hunt and gather food and collect wood for their families.

Jordan Crugnale

Foreword

Manungka Manungka Women's Association, incorporated under the Aboriginal Associations Act, was originally formed in 1985 as the Desert Women's Project at the specific request of a large group of Senior Law Women from Balgo (Wirrimanu), Billiluna, Malarn and Ringers Soak (Kundat Djaru). The project commenced in February 1987 when funding was achieved and a Co-ordinator was employed. The need of these Law women for support in the maintenance of their traditional cultural activities, plus their desire for a medium through which they could have access and input on contemporary issues, led to the creation of the Desert Women's Project.

The power and status of Women's law in these communities received scant acknowledgement, recognition or respect from European organisations. Women's Law is the concern of women alone. It was, and still is, inappropriate for Law women to present their concerns to men and unknown government and non-government officials.

The women's silence was often taken as acquiescence or disinterest on issues of community concern. The Law Women are generally illiterate, with limited English language skills. When it was appropriate for them to speak it was difficult to make their voices heard. Consequently the women were not provided with the services and facilities they needed. Many community resources became monopolised by the men. Contrary to traditional practice the women were dependent upon the men for the fulfilment of their cultural activities.

Manungka Manungka supports the Western Desert women by implementing projects and activities which maintain women's culture as a

living, dynamic and relevant force. The Association provides resources such as motor vehicles — which allow the women to hunt,
travel for women's business and to maintain ceremonial links with
country — and audio and video equipment to record stories, songs
and dance. Manungka Manungka also organises training as the
women request, such as driving lessons, photography, audio and
video operation, batik and silk screening.

To promote greater understanding of Western Desert women's
culture through the Association, the women have travelled interstate
and overseas to share their song, dance and painting with the wider
community. Manungka Manungka is also a conduit for information
on such matters as mining, government legislation, nutrition and
health, which allows the women to once again make the informed
decisions about their lives and let their voices be heard.

Michelle Mackenzie
Co-ordinator 1989—1992

MANUNGKA
MANUNGKA
WOMEN'S ASSOCIATION

Contents

Introduction

We want people to learn about our culture
We got a lot of stories...secret ones too
Too long people not listening to women
Not listening to Aboriginal people

We women got our own Law and Culture
Different from men
We not stupid
Giving you very important stories about our culture
So you people understand
We wanna spread our stories down to Perth...and other side
Overseas too...right around

Our children wanna be learning our stories
Keep on hanging onto our culture
Keep it strong
Listen to what women saying
It very important

We getting old now
We worrying for mining companies
They think we stupid
Treat us with no respect for Culture and Law
Government mob too
We know how to look after our country
It very special to us
You'll see
You'll understand

Ngunytja Napanangka Mosquito

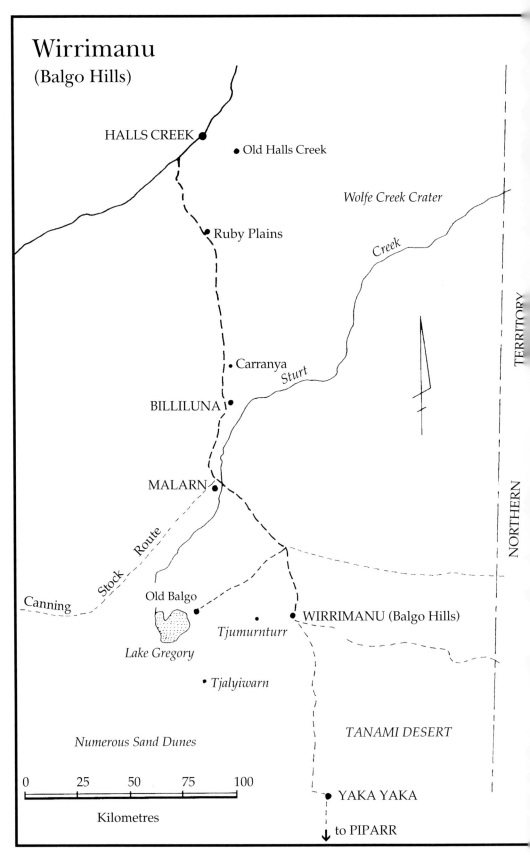

Wirrimanu
(Balgo Hills)

HALLS CREEK

● Old Halls Creek

Wolfe Creek Crater

Creek

● Ruby Plains

● Carranya

Sturt

BILLILUNA

MALARN

Stock Route

Canning

Old Balgo

● WIRRIMANU (Balgo Hills)

Tjumurnturr

Lake Gregory

● *Tjalyiwarn*

TANAMI DESERT

Numerous Sand Dunes

NORTHERN TERRITORY

| 0 | 25 | 50 | 75 | 100 |

Kilometres

● YAKA YAKA

to PIPARR

STORIES TOLD BY

Lumu Nungurrayi

TRANSLATED BY

Marri Nakamarra Matjital
Tjama Napanangka

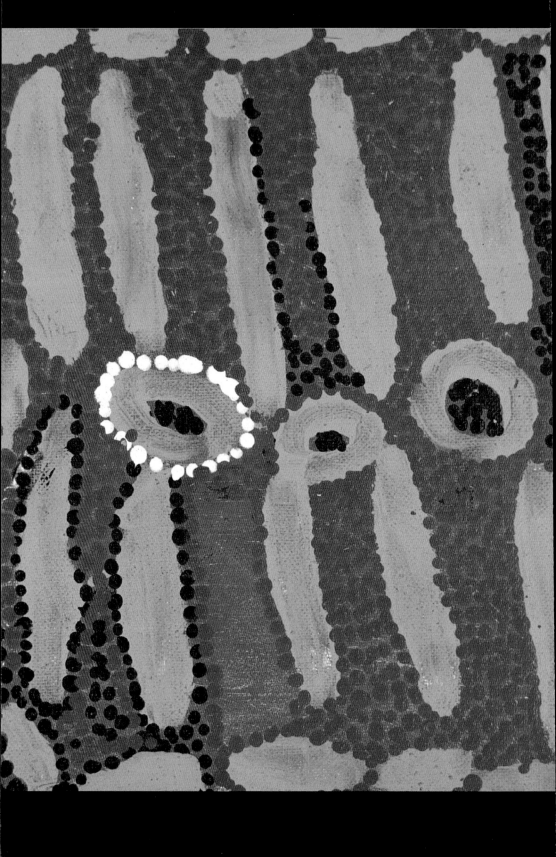

It's collecting time

It was that time of the year to collect seeds and berries again
Black and brown seeds were ready
Lukararra, warupunyu…
The women all went out bush to get them
Fill the coolamons and cleaning it
Then take it back to the main camp
They grind it and put bush damper on the hot coals and sand
Everybody shared that damper
They go walkabout again and collecting more food.

Old people stay at camp and look after grandchildren
Grandmothers cook for the children
They used to get two rocks and start grinding seeds
Give them to the children and some old people who are blind
The women came back with meat and berries
The hunters shared the food with old people and children
After eating everybody go to sleep
Then everybody move to the other rockhole and make camp
The hunters went walkabout again
Children stayed with the old people
We hunted lots of bush berries and seeds and meat.

The rockhole there was called Kitjilyiilyi
We went all over the place
It was the rain season and we were all happy
The rain will make black seeds grow again, berries will come up too
Lots of green grass for the kangaroos and other animals.

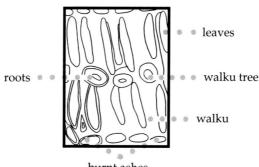

roots

leaves

walku tree

walku

burnt ashes

We start going walkabout again and get berries and seeds
Put them in our coolamons and take them back to camp
The black seeds was main food
For Aboriginal people in those days
We would store them until next winter
They grow during the rain and ready to collect in the winter.

We moved to another rockhole and made camp there
The men went hunting and the women went walkabout
The old people stayed in the camp
Taking care of the children and the blind people
Everybody had to go back to the big rockhole Kitjilyiilyi
No water in the new rockhole
It was back to the rockhole which was our birth place
We went walkabout and hunting again.

Helping out

Sometimes a man helped his wife get those black seeds and berries. She was a pregnant woman. He pulled out some grass seeds and put them next to his wife. She separated the grass, dirt and leaves from the good seeds. Then the husband went out hunting again to get meat for the family. The men share meat with everybody and the woman share the food as well. The men hunted kangaroos, emu, rabbits, turkey, cat and wallaby, goanna.

The women collected bush berries, bush nuts, bush potatoes, bush onions, seeds, tomatoes and bush carrots. They also collected wood for cooking and to keep them warm in the winter. They build little shelters with some grass, sticks and antbed. My parents taught me how to hunt for bushtucker.

Bushtucker is very special to us and we ate all of it, we never wasted any. Our grandparents and parents taught us that and to always share our tucker in the desert. When we growing up we went walkabout to collect berries and seeds. That is how I came to be a good hunter.

We travelled to another waterhole and went walkabout again. The men hunted for meat and they sometimes speared a kangaroo and cooked it out bush. When it was cooked the men cut it and share the meat to take back to their families. We stayed at this rockhole for long time…Multju rockhole. We had lots of bushtucker and people came from everywhere to camp at this rockhole. It was big water and it was there all during summer. That my place and my family's…it was a good place. It on the Canning Stock Route, other side of Nyarurri.

The men went hunting and sometimes took the wife so she can collect some berries and dig for potato. The children stayed with the grandparents. We lived on bushtucker and the women used to grind seeds and share it out. The mother teaches the children the new bushtucker and when she cooks it, we all try it.

The people used to dig for soakwater and it was clean and fresh for drinking. When everyone finish drinking the man gets some sticks and leaves to cover it because of the animals. Sometimes the little birds make toilet in the soakwater and it go green, get dirty.

The little kids stay at camp with the grannies and the big ones go out bush so that they can be taught. The mother takes the girls and shows them how to follow tracks and dig the animal out of a hole. She teaches them to eat a grasshopper and how to collect bush-seeds…if it's too green it not ready. When the seeds brown and black they are ready. Mother tells them that when the tomato is white and yellow, it is ready to eat, and not green. The men showed the boys how to hunt.

In the afternoon the grannies tell the little children that their brothers and sisters are coming back with lots of food. The kids watch out from the little sandhills near the main camp. When they see their family they get really happy and run to tell the grannies. The grannies light a fire and cook the meat. When the meat cooks, they give it to the boys to eat. The boys tell the grandma that she can have some.
Yeah, I'll have some.
The rest of the meat goes to the family.

The next day he went out again and tells his grandmother that he'll kill more meat for her but she gotta make damper. The grandma feel proud when she heard her grandson speak to her. Mothers and fathers take their children out hunting again. Back at the camp the grandmothers and other children get two rocks ready for grinding them black seeds to make that damper.

Some hunters come back with a cooked kangaroo and they share it out. The people ate everything from the kangaroo meat and they also chop the bone to get the inside fat.

The husband likes to take his wife out hunting and leave the kids behind with the grandparents in case they can collect extra bushtucker. The father and mother collected enough food for the family and everybody had plenty to eat. They ate and ate and ate and had some in the morning for breakfast.

Sometimes when people used to go camping they light a bushfire. It mean signal, to get rid of the old bushtucker so when it rains the next year the new ones come up good. One man came and lit a fire and everyone knew someone was coming. When he came closer the people started crying and all sat around him. His aunty told him to stay with her and she would take care of him. When he was grown up he was married there. He took his wife to another camp because another man was after the young woman.

When the young woman was pregnant she stayed with a mother until she had the baby. The midwife was her grandmother and she stayed with her until the baby was strong. The husband not allowed to see that baby or mother. Baby gotta be smoked first. He can't even see the place the baby was born. Husband sends her food with the grandmother. It was time for the mother to show the baby to the father and the rest of the family. The mother and father take the baby wherever they go…camping, hunting and walkabout.

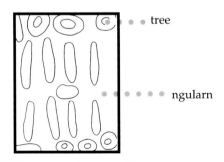

Fill him up coolamon p. 8

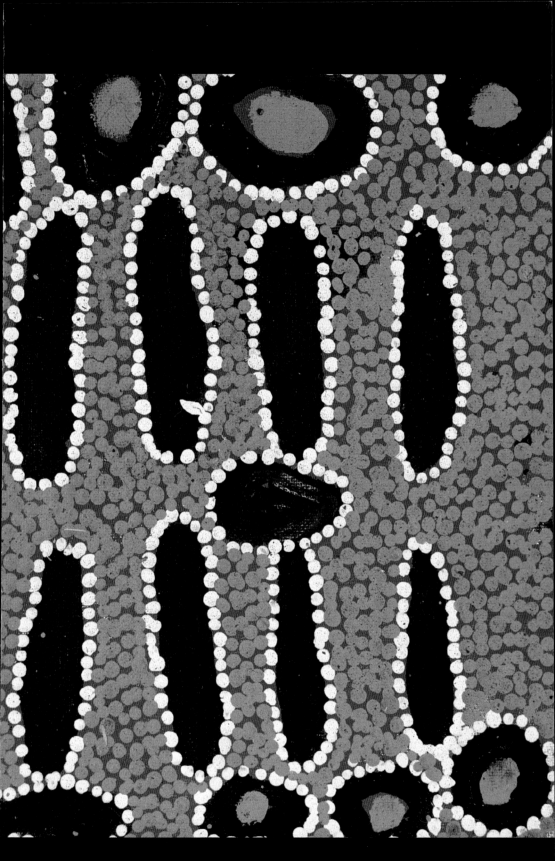

Story p. 8

The man went hunting with his spears and boomerang and killed lots of animals, cooked it, and ate and ate. The woman knows how to take the guts out from the kangaroo and goanna. The family all have a good feed, eating meat and sharing. The people went again, hunting meat and collecting bushtucker.

At home we cook all the food at the sametime and put some away for the morning. It was wintertime and our mob still went hunting but couldn't find any tracks…the goannas were all asleep for the winter. The women collected seeds and other bushtucker. We bin put seeds in coolamon, different ones in each, stack them all up and put them in tree. It rations for wintertime. Birds don't eat them…we cover them up. Only one family live in that area so no one ever steal them. We travelling around…not many people. Might be two men, sisters for the men, kids, mothers, two old grannies and old man. The men and women killed lots of meat. The women cooked for everyone and shared it out. In the morning the father and mother go hunting again. Everyone helps out.

Keep going

That old woman bin look after little baby, that mother one go hunting. That little baby at home on self. Mother bin go out getting wallaby, hunting around then bring home, cook and eat it. Mother bin put windbreak for that little baby and she bin go hunting around. Granny bin look after baby. Mother one bin go hunting getting all them wallaby. He bring it home and cook it and give it to granny and little kid. They bin leave some for morning. That kid grown up little bit, crawling, and that granny still look after that kid.

It summertime. Granny bin give only little pieces of food, kid nearly walk now. Mother and granny bin feed that kid. That little kid bin go hunting around for lizard not far from camp. Mother and granny bin happy for that kid. They bin go to another place and on road husband and wife bin go hunting. Granny bin go behind with kid. Too much they bin kill them animals, fat ones too. Come back afternoon, have dinner out…granny looking after kid. Husband and wife come back with lot of food.

Husband and wife bin come out to another place, big mob people living there. Granny and baby, he big now, bin go there too. They bin fill up coolamon plenty animal, and bin share that food out with all the people.

Old granny bin have big family, lot of grand kids. All the families go to another place.

That husband go hunting self and the wife go get bushtucker. They bin come back with plenty animals and bushtucker. All little kids watching for mother and father to come back. Them kids really hungry and that mother bin give them cooked wallaby. They all bin share them out. All the kids and grannies ate all night, they not leaving some for tomorrow. Sometime they camp two days eating lot of food. That husband and wife tell everyone they go hunting after lunch.

Two fella bin go in the afternoon and come back with big mob of food. They bin have it for supper and leave some for morningtime. Husband and wife bin have lot of children and the girls bin give away to marry. The youngest too shy to get marry. Can't talk, she promised.

One man had two of the daughters. The three went hunting and that man bin kill animals and the girls bin get bushtucker. Man bin go look for two girls and they bin make fire and cook all the food. They bin bring it home later, cooked. Man bin tell wives to take some food to mother and father. That husband of the two girls really good hunter. They bin make big damper for daughters, cousins and granny. Cut half, half, half…share it for everyone.

Morningtime they bin go out hunting, that man and two wives, have dinner out. They bin come back next day with cooked meat and bring it home for everyone to eat. Everyone bin leave some pussycat for morning and that granny bin eating all night.

Morningtime we go to another place, he wintertime now. Get bushtucker, like plum, and fellas go hunting. Halfway, they found tucker and everyone fill him up coolamon. Man go front. They bin find waterhole, sit there and have bushtucker and drink water too. They bin eating white tomato too much. Get more, fill him up and leave for after. Two days eating bushtucker then keep going to another place.

Fill him up coolamon

We start walking to another place, getting all the animals all the way. Morningtime go hunting again, killing all the animals. Sometimes we bin go and get bushtucker. Man bin go out for goanna and get plenty wayurta, brush tail possum one.

Summertime we bin get some white seeds, waral waral, fill him up coolamon, save for that raintime. Bin find things under spinifex, like little spinifex…take it and grind him on stone. Use that seeds for damper. Fill him up, put in heap, grind him up and then put in coolamon to sort out rubbish ones.

All the way we bin fill him up, take home to make damper for the children. Some fella they leave morningtime, go out and fill him up again. That bushtucker finish he go underground. We go get different one, round one, kanytjilyi — that bush raisin. They wetten him and put in coolamon, make him soft, then cook big damper. Sometime man go out, get all animals…women go separate and fill him up bushtucker and bring it home to camp, cook it and share it out.

After finish we bin go to another soakwater. We bin eating any type of bushtucker waiting for tomatoes. No coldsick in bush, we bin grow up on good food.

Summertime we have that yellow flowers from tree, it like honey. Sometime we go early early in morning, get that ngularn and we bin fill him up coolamon. We put ashes in coolamon and put under tree and put sugar on top. He feeling nice and soft and then take him back to camp.

Sun get up, finish, no more sugar. Have to get him early early. Sun up, won't find him, only find bushes and leaves. Wintertime we bin get white sugar and summertime them yellow flowers.

We bin go to another living water for more bush honey. When that one finish we all change over to big tree, fill him up. It like lollies. Sometime we go out with the round coolamon and get spinifex and water. Put spinifex in water with that sugar, soak him and then suck it. It like ice lolly.

Man and woman break that leaf, you know, and take him home and put him in water to soak. Everyone does it. Sometime people go hunting and put that yurrany in water, sweet one, and eat on the way. Kids go get bushtucker, break that leaf and give it to granny, he put in water.

We go to another place, look for more sugar…we finish them. We bin run looking for water, and they right, that rockhole he full. We bin find more yurrany. Fill him up coolamon, bin fill right up and give to them two grannies. Sometime mothers bin put that tucker in sun to dry and sometime leave it for tomorrow.

After that water wash away, finish, and go look around for more. Mothers bin find some kanytjilyi. They greedy ones, they bin eat whole lot. Sometime they bin find that white tomato, after that sugar finish, that water bin wash him away. Fill him up bush tomato, take home and eat it.

From there we start walk to another waterhole, look around for more bush tomato. Fill him up more. Mans bin go out hunting, bin bring back kangaroos and lizards. Mothers bin cook that kuka in fire and after, pull him out, cut him up and give liver to old womans. They happy for that liver. Old ladies bin get head, tail and that back bone and they real happy. They bin feed blind woman too, and soon as they all finish they go to sleep. Old woman bin look after that blind one. Go hunting holding his arm — true. Two fella go sit down, make windbreak and fire.

We were real skinny ones in bush — fast too. Anyone can grab that kangaroo's tail, even the girls. Different food in the bush. We bin chase and kill animals when we kids, we really quick. Bin get pussycat, wallaby, goanna and little kangaroos. It all changed now. We dying from sugar…early too. We bin have different training in bush, bin go without meat and food for one months. Take long time to die…

Hunting all the way

When I was a little girl
All the kids bin walk around
All bin come back to mother
Look around for lizard
Sometime all us little kids went hunting
Killing little lizard, bring home, cook and eat it
Mother and father go hunting separate
Come back afternoontime.

Go to another place in morning
Kill goanna all the way
Come out to another soakwater
Living there.

Summertime
Bushtucker fill him up coolamon
Get seed from spinifex grass
Fill him up coolamon
Grind it and make damper
Bin get brown seed and wet him in water
We call that seed…warupunyu
Leave till morning, let him get soak
Get up and try grind him. It's right, soft one
All grinding making damper
Two big one, two little one
Them big one we bin make for the men
All bin go to another place, no water
Big mob people bin finish it
We bin go to another waterhole, have dinner
Then bin go hunting and getting plenty.

Morningtime go out again, go light fire
After that, kill goannas
Big fire, cook it and take it home
They bin cover up bushes to hide animals
That eagle won't get them animals.

All young boys playing around, laughing all night
They bin telling funny stories
Boys go hunting
They go, cook it and leave for morning
Bring home for mother and father
Give it to them
We go to another place, living there.

Grubs encountered during yam digging

STORIES TOLD BY

Marri Yakuny Napurrula

TRANSLATED BY

Tjama Napanangka

Camping all the way

I bin take my granny Nangala, she blind one, no fire, camping at Murtulyu. We bin travelling from Manga Manga to Kurtulyuparri. After that, to Warumunily. We bin pass that way and sat down in the sun. My granny pass away, I bin lose her there.

From there I bin travelling and see fire long long way, start heading that way and camp halfway with no fire. Morningtime start walk byself to that fire. I bin come out and get happy, I bin see a camp, they all here. I bin tell them that I bin lose my granny and they bin start crying for that lady.

We bin then stop at Lawa Lawa, other side Walkarli, bit west, and get plenty carrots and yams. Then we go to Tjirtirr rockhole. From there bin start walk to another place, Mungayawu. Then we go to Yurrumarraly, other side of Putja, north. We bin go for karnti, them bush potatoes.

I was little girl. We bin see white man on camel.
Wara? we bin say. *What's that?*
We all bin run away. We didn't know white man. First time we see him.

Those kartiya knew that language. Braitling, that fella name. They bin come out and make tea for us. Old ladies bin get spinifex, put in that funny cup, soak it, take it out and suck it. They never use that cup. Then we all bin run away, run to Kaningara and bin living there. That white man keep going Canning Stock Route. We all bin living together, Wangkajunga and Walmajarri people.

From there we bin find cheeky animal. That animal bin jump on me and bite me all over. I bin cry hard, all over blood. I bin go home and all bin ask me who did that bite. I bin tell them it was cheeky and man bin go and kill him. They bin tell me it called kalany. That short black wallaby.

We bin get tjurnta, that bush onion, fill him up coolamon and go back to camp in Pulka, Parakura side. After, we all went back again for that bush onion. Then we bin go to Manga Manga and some fellas bin stay there.

You fella can go by self, we go get bushtucker.
Stop at Manga Manga. Some went to get tucker in Pulka. They all
bin sit down and waiting for mother to come back.

Sometime all the little kid go hunting and get little lizard and
carrots, waiting for mother to come back in morningtime. Mother
they come back and look at all kids.
Ahhhh, they all still alive.
We all happy, big mob of wallabies and bush onions, plenty feed
for all the kids.

Back at Manga Manga for different bushtucker. We go up and
down, up and down. Then we bin shift to Walkarli and we bin go
up and Yurrumarraly and camp halfway, hunting for tjirrilpatja,
bush carrots in Putja, that place.

We bin go to Kantawarra, Watjangarti, Kayarla…big rockhole,
getting bushtucker on the way. We bin living there for a while,
have plenty tucker, yams, carrots, seeds.

What about we go other side?
No, we gotta finish all this bushtucker first, live here first.
Come on we go…
No we stop here.

Later we bin go to Lanu Lanu. We bin see bullock. All bin come
from bush, first time I bin see that animal. We go back — white
man frighten us, he might kill us, shoot us. We bin go back home
fast. Plenty tucker there. We gotta go that way to Walyatjirra. We go
to Tjipirr and then to Tjiitjinganngarr.

We bin finish that bushtucker before the rain. We head off to
another waterhole and make windbreak. It bin raining all night. At
Kurtulyuparri we bin make big mob of damper, bushtucker everywhere. We bin talk about going back to Manga Manga, and we bin
go. We bin have plenty of that black seed mungily. We wash him
out salt — grind him, taste him…no salt. They bin get that
bushtucker, black one, fill him up coolamon and we bin make too
much damper.

Somebody bin light fire and we all bin look.
Somebody coming!
How many?
I don't know.
We got plenty bush carrots and too much damper. Man bin come, Payi Payi husband, Tjampitjin. Some young boys bin have big fight. Some other people bin come from Tjalyiwarn, that Mosquito, Ngunytja husband now. We bin living at Wangkatjungka.

Our mob bin got to Wangkatji, this side Lanu Lanu, but little bit east, and bin living there. Some bin go Canning Stock Route, separate from us. Then we bin come to Tjalyiwarn and from there to Kunawarawara, where we bin have plenty bushtucker. After that we light fire for roughtail lizard. Go back to Yurrumarraly, long way, and we all bin living there.

From Tjiipaly we bin go to camp halfway and keep going morning-time, back to my country. Somebody light fire, somebody coming. Anyway we stay at Tjiipaly. All the Walmajarri people bin come out at Tjiipaly and they bin ask us which way they gotta go for bush-tucker. We bin tell them to go That Way.

Start again to another place, Kumpuwaljta, and camp there one night, keep going to another place. We all bin go on that same road to the same place…up and down, up and down.

Twin Lakes near Yaka Yaka

Watikutjarra south of Yaka Yaka

STORIES TOLD BY

Milyika Napaltjarri

TRANSLATED BY

Tangayi Napurrula
Marri Nakamarra Matjital
Tjama Napanangka

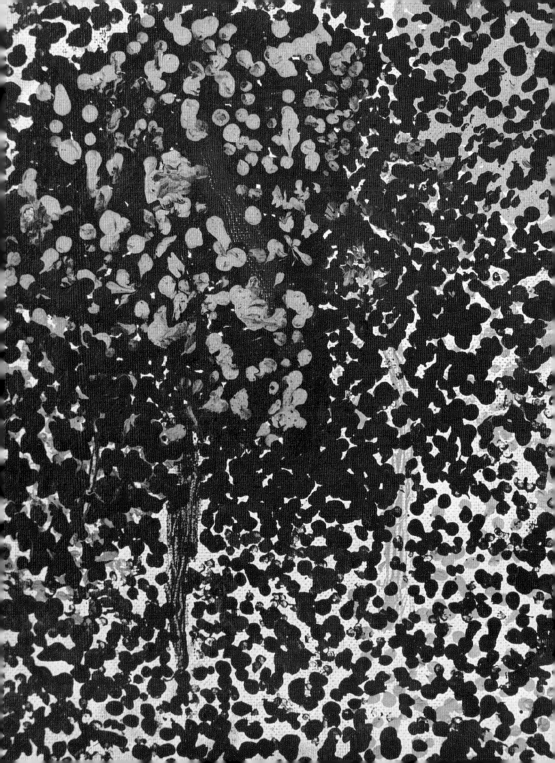

Walking around with my mother

My mother and other women used to go hunting, getting their own food, and us mob went to get our own too. This is when we were young girls and we get plenty of bushtucker. My sisters taught me to go hunting. My sisters taught me about Law and Culture.

When my mother come back from hunting they used to get lots of bushtucker and the bushtucker was walku. They used to make a big fire and cook it. We used that plum to rub our hair to make it long...make hair grow fast. We were waiting for our mothers and fathers to come home from hunting. We used to squeeze it and rub all over body.

For Culture, while we were waiting, we used to put tucker on our bodies. All the young girls used our mothers' ochre when they went out hunting. We used to make big fire to cook that walku. We also used to cook mangarta on the fire, and from the fire it would open when cooked. We used to rub that quandong all over us...it was very greasy. When our mothers come back from hunting they bin ask:
Look at these girls, what they bin doing? They bin using this one here, walku and mangarta.

Our mothers would go out to get karrulykura, wangki, nyurrariku. They used to get plenty, not far from camp. They get big mob. Get just tucker, no leaves, used to get plenty of tucker on that trees, biggest mob. That karrulykura is like a bag in the tree made by an insect. Our country had this kind of tucker, never go short of tucker, plenty there. I wouldn't know which way to go to get tucker...it was everywhere.

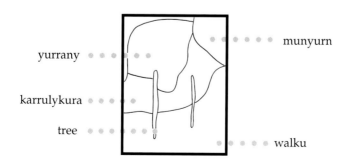

All the young girls, no boys, would stay at camp and their mothers would come back and say: *Are you all right?*
And happy to see them that nothing happened. I would go out hunting with all the other girls and learn to get our own food. Sometimes all the young girls would get leaves to make a shelter.

Mother would come back and we bin get up and stand in a line: *What bin happening? What you bin doing?*
We tell her that we bin using this one here…that mangarta, same one. We all bin start laughing. Mother bin bring back lot of goanna, rabbit and meow. We used to get happy when we bin see them coming.

When mothers come back from hunting we used to sit down with big mob goanna, blue tongue, and pink one like that blue tongue. Our mothers would start painting themselves and when we see other people with big goanna, we would go over and sit with them, so they would give us some. That bushtucker bin share with everyone.

Dig up more

We went for hunting
Got lots of bush potatoes
Cooked and ate them
I was a young girl
Then we lay down to have a rest after eating
We wait till we get hungry
Had some in the fire under the coals
Raw ones in the coolamon too
After that, we go hunting again to dig up more
We got more and someone said:
How can we eat all this?
All our coolamons were full up.

We went back to the place where some were cooking
Had lunch there
Tea, water and bush potato
We were all tired from digging
Had a big rest.

The ones cooking lunch and looking after camp
Their turn to go and dig for potatoes
They take out the cook ones and put more in
They kept some for those out hunting
And for the children back at Wirrimanu
Put them…put, put, put…in them coolamons.

Some other women went hunting for goanna
The others were getting bush potato
Save some potato for the women who will give us goanna.

When the woman go for a walk
They find lots of bush potato plant
So they start looking for little cracks in the ground
They look near the plant so they can start digging
They know where the potato is
Every woman had their own coolamon
When they went digging they take all the potatoes out of the hole
Don't leave any, they might go rotten.

I ate lots of cooked potatoes and I didn't give it to anyone
When I was young I never share that tucker
I'm not greedy
Now I am old I share it — true.

Mother didn't help us

Bin go out and get that nyuwari bushtucker
Get him, light fire with spinifex and cook whole lot
We bin get it from tree
Squeeze him…eat him raw
He black one, like plum
We get them separate
I'm big enough to get bushtucker by self
We take them home to camp
Cook some up and put seeds in hair
Mother don't help us, get on self
Living big mob people
Getting plenty tucker everywhere we go.

Soon as we bin grow big
We bin going out getting goanna
Never with mother
Bin go separate way.

We bin go out getting eggs from ants
We no worry about mother, go by self
Ant eggs, big mob of white eggs
Same time bin get purarra…that honey ant.

Out hunting we bin get stick…stick for digging
Bin make it sharp one
Mother didn't help us.

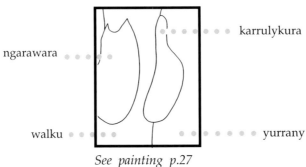

See painting p.27

Go get like a coolamon, bark one
Never get anything till I got woman
Bin living on purarra
Sometime go hunting, digging hole
He might be there
Digging for that bushtucker.

Get something like honey
He under tree, hand goes in under the ground
Ants…hard work digging that hole for that honey
Get some, take home, share it out.

White one like onions, puluntari
When animals have them they get weak
Good for people
Animals can't walk.

Everyone bin give me food

My mother tell me I gotta eat it, good tucker
I know now
People don't like it first time
I try him
I don't like…but he right now.

My sisters bin feed me something
They bin look after me
They find me another bushtucker, round thing…wangki
That kumputjirr, we get it and put in antbed
Squash him on that flat antbed
Get too full, go toilet from that bushtucker
Soon as we squeeze him, comes water
Then dry him in sun
Like a raisin.

Tjaakarmpa, black one, look from long way
Too many hanging down on tree, like bush currant
Run and get him, fill him up coolamon
Happy…we got plenty tucker

Others bin tell me to share them:
You can't finish them one, you gotta share him out
Too much for one.

Shake that tree, they fall over
Fill him up coolamon with currants
Cut that tree little bit, them fall
Shake, shake…fall over from tree on ground.

We go hunting by self, separate and pick up bushtucker
No mother, go self
Mother go different way, hunting around
Man give goanna to womans
Womans give them bushtucker.

After that we go hunting for wartingkurra
Get big mob, fill up coolamon
I don't worry about other tucker
They take it and make fire
Cook it really hot, take out of fire
Bin living on wartingkurra.

Warnintji, he small insect, like ant
Every raintime he go to house, see that light
We catch him and cook him in fire in ground.

Walk around…no rags, no clothes
Bin wearing hairbelts
Bin move to another place
Living in Yintjinti.

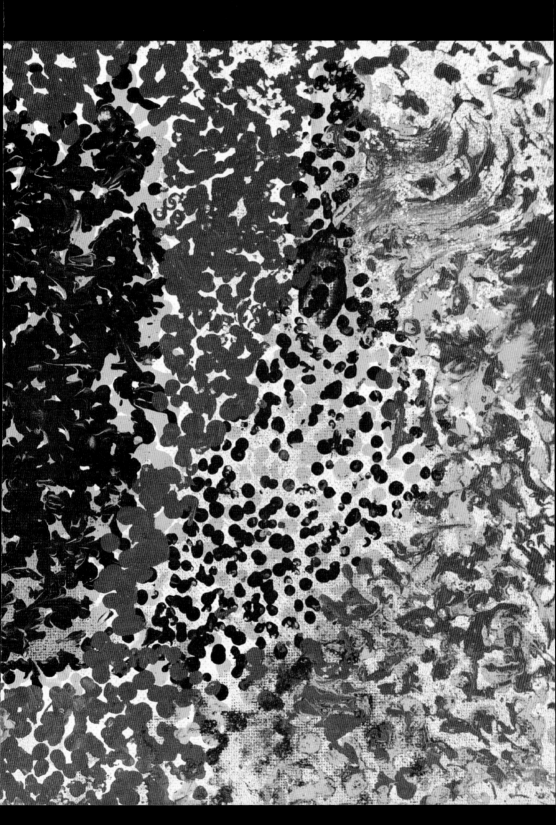

See key p. 24

STORIES TOLD BY

Nancy Kungkulu Tax

TRANSLATED BY

Rhonda Tax
Marri Nakamarra Matjital
Tjama Napanangka

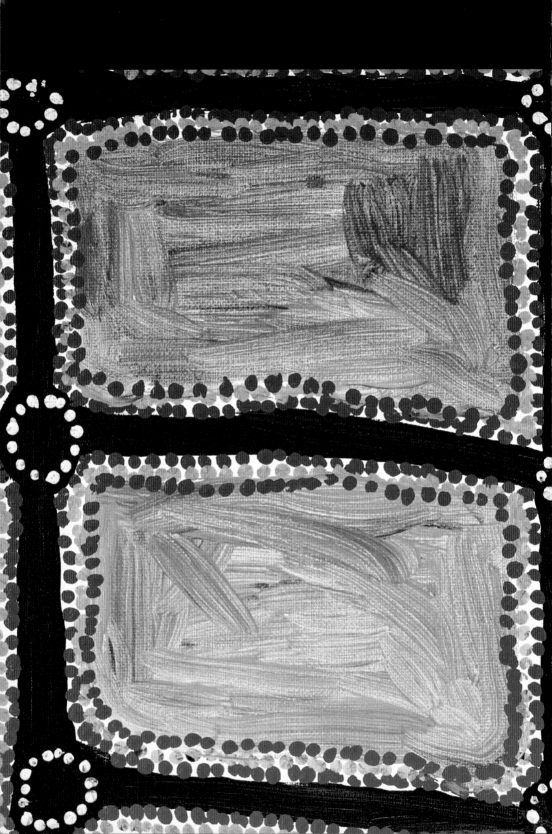

In the bush

I lived with my grandmother in the bush when I was little. My
mother ran off with another husband. I had to stay with her.
We started walking through Lake Gregory, Kilang Kilang, and
turned left to go to Lampu Well. That was the last water and so we
had little and camped in the middle of the dry desert. We still had
water in those big coolamon on our heads. We keep going, heading
for Tangku.

During the middle of the day, we all sat down in the shade for a rest
and wait for the sun to go down, wait for it to get little bit cooler.
Then we start again. We camped just near Ngaranytjartu, then we
arrive there. We tasted the water, it was a well, and it was very salty.
So we keep going looking for another water. We found a rockhole,
little bit wet, no water in it so the people started digging then clean
it and wait for the water to come up. We filled our coolamons and
kept going and camp halfway on the road. Some sat in the shade
and some kept going because they knew where the water was. The
men went in front with some kids and we stayed behind; grandmother and us were tired. The first mob found water and had to dig
for soakwater. They waited for the others and when we got there we
camped for two-three days.

We started walking again in the morning and saw some people in
Tangku. People looking after sheep there. For those who were looking after sheep, people would bring more load of food for them on
horse, no mutika then, in those days. When we arrived to the main
camp, everyone was painted up so we painted up, sorry meeting.
Both groups of men threw boomerangs and everyone was crying.

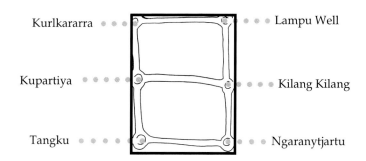

Kurlkararra •••   ••• Lampu Well

Kupartiya ••••   ••• Kilang Kilang

Tangku ••••   ••• Ngaranytjartu

Some people used to steal the sheep and eat it. No one knew. (I laugh because they used to do that at Old Mission, when I was a big girl, and the police used to come). Our mob stole kartiya food at Tangku when we were passing through but they never catch us.

Then we went our own way. I went to Kupartiya (Bohemia), with my granny. Some went to Christmas Creek, some to Fitzroy. We kept going from Kupartiya to Kurlkarrara and got there at night and made camp. Some went to say hello to the people who lived there and they gave them food. It was the best time at night to sneak to the house where the main camp was and let them know how many people are travelling. They were afraid of white man.

In the morning we left early and as we walked along, some men and women went hunting and killed big water goannas, quite different from the ones in the desert. We had been travelling all day along the big river and we stopped in the afternoon to make camp.

Morningtime we had breakfast and rolled the swags and started walking again. As we walked some people killed goannas and cooked them for everybody. We continued on and arrived at Margaret River after travelling around Louisa Downs, Mary River. We don't get tired like in the desert, lots of water, can swim, and we were happy. The people there greeted us and gave us rations …kartiya was good. We had Christmas and New Year there. After New Year we had to travel again and kartiya gave us food to take with us.

We were travelling back the same way we came, same story, stopping halfway, camping out and walking. We went straight to Kupartiya. My real father stayed at this place, and we went to Christmas Creek. When we arrived people were down near the river, not at the house. Some started working here, those travelling nomad people. People worked in the bush making tanks, yards, fences and when they finished they come back to the station for Christmas.

We left Christmas Creek and headed for Cherrabun. We camped halfway and had lunch halfway. The next day we got to the station. We saw lot of Walmajarri people. We left and headed north to

Jubilee Downs. We stayed there for a while and then headed back to Cherrabun and got there at night-time, not too far. No mutika... long time ago.

We went back to get our grandmother at Cherrabun, she had to stay with some family. Then we all started walking back to Christmas Creek. When we were travelling to this creek, we saw stockmen on the way.

I saw my real father working in the stockyard. Then I went back to my mother and stepfather. I had to travel with them. Kartiya gave us rations at Christmas Creek and we left to go on holiday to a camp in the bush. Kartiya used to bring us rations every week. We had three months and kartiya told us to go bush for that time.

It was time for us to go back to the station to start work. We made tanks, build yards, fences and some men were working on the stock-yards, mustering bullocks and horses. When people were working out in the bush they had contract and each week someone from the group would go to the main camp to get rations.

Walk...camp...walk...camp

Mother and father pick us up, the two daughters, at Cherrabun and we went to Jubilee Station. After that we went back to the bush, the whole family. We went through the hill near Christmas Creek, then to Tangku and killed kangaroo with a spear. We kept going through the desert through Ngaranytjartu. We ate lots of food when we were travelling. We camped at Lampu Well, then at Kilang Kilang near the lake. We ate only meat, no other bush food. The people from Balgo came this way for hunting. Old Mission people saw tracks near Kurntukuta but we keep going to Old Billiluna.

We camped there. My real father died at Kupartiya, I was travelling with my second father. We went to Old Billiluna Station, that's Lake Stretch, but no one was there. We went to new Billiluna and saw people there, some working in the stockyard.

We went back

Me and my husband went to Taapayi, stayed all afternoon and then went to Kunawarawara rockhole, this side of Tjalyiwarn. Got to Tjalyiwarn, stayed for a few weeks and went back. Had no more tucker, went back for more rations; wheat flour, sugar, tea, tobacco.

We had some kuka for lunch and went on same road. Camped one night at rockhole, that Kunawarawara one, and got to Old Balgo in the afternoon. We had no mutika, walked all the way. In Old Balgo we got our rations and went back out, carrying our swags, billycans and tent.

We sat under the trees, then went straight to that rockhole and soakwater. Got our billycans of water, carry them, to go hunting. We stayed one week out in the bush and back again hunting and getting bush food.

Looking for parents

Me and my husband went back to Billiluna to look for his mother. When we were young we walked, we didn't have any children then. We left Old Balgo and we camped at Old Station. In the morning we kept on walking and came to a place called Palapiyarru (only a yard between Billiluna and Malarn). We killed goannas and got bushtucker.

When we got there, his parents were not there. They were out making fences working for kartiya on stock camps. People told us they were making new stockyards at Tjangalatjarra windmill. We stayed down the river at the bushcamp with Jaru, Ngarti and Walmajarri people, waiting for his parents to return. They came in for the weekend to get more rations for everyone working on contract at the yards. This way they had a chance to meet the relations. The people on contract got more things than people on the river. The workers got more food, got blankets, swags, hats. We stayed there for a holiday then started walking back.

On the way back we had no donkeys or cars for carrying swags and
we never got sick, we were really healthy. The sun was going
down…we got to Old Balgo, the mission. It was near the river and
there were humpies everywhere along the riverbed. We didn't have
houses, we had to make our own tents, humpies, windbreaks,
spinifex houses. No kartiya building…nothing.

In the morning, we went to get our rations. Then we went out hunting for the day and some people looking after sheeps and some
after goats. In the afternoon we came home with goannas for the
family and for the two Napurrulas, Nanyuma and Marri Yakuny. Big
rain came and we didn't have a humpy, we covered ourselves with
our canvasses.

Fight

The women and men started mustering camels at Billiluna. The
stockmen went ahead with the cattle and horses and the cooks rode
with the camels and swags on top. We met at camp, at Kurtu
soakwater, and the stockmen went mustering there.

Then someone told the boss that my husband was riding the same
horse. They had a fight (my husband and that kartiya). My husband
broke his jaw, so we went east to Balgo and camp halfway. We had
food that the cookie gave us and we had to walk, finish work. We had
breakfast on the way and kept going east to Balgo, killing goannas
for food. We chop trees to get witchetty grubs. We had lunch, then
keep going. We camped at Pankupiti, near Malarn and morningtime
we walked through lake at Malarn, no water in it then. We keep
going and camped at Kurntukuta. Next day we keep walking…
walking…walking.

At night we got to Balgo. We could hear voices everywhere talking.
We heard a voice of the family and saw Nanyuma and baby
Napangarti (Patricia Milner). All the dogs start barking and the
people knew that strangers or visitors or relatives were here. They
said hello to us and asked how we got here.
We walked, I said.
And we lived here at Old Mission just because of a fight with a white
man. Living there for good now.

Kid trouble

We had a son in Balgo
We went hunting for goannas
I was carrying Ronnie on my shoulders and he fell off
But I didn't tell my husband
We sat in the shade, had a drink of water
Then we started hunting goannas again
After that we had to sit in the shade and make fire
Cook our food
I left my baby sleeping to go get wood
All the ants were biting him
His father was laying down beside him and didn't notice
I had to scream to him from far away
Baby was crying
I told my husband:
Why didn't you look after the baby?
I started shaking them off.

We ate the food
Then left the shade and started walking back to Balgo
We gave some goanna to Marri Yakuny Napurrula
In the morning
We all went to get our rations from Fr Alphonse
Then we all went camping out at Tjirrtjirr
In the morning we went to another waterhole,
Shifting camp, Kupartalangu.

The baby was sick at this place
Me and my husband had to take the baby to hospital in Balgo
The nurse had to pull it out, something in his throat
Sister pulled out a piece of grass and duck's eggshell
Must have got stuck from drinking water from the rockhole
Sister gave him some medicine.

Then we left and went camping again
We cooked goannas and ate them again
Then we ran out of flour, tea and sugar

Back to Balgo again for more rations
Next day we went back out camping
Killed goannas again
Those people were really good at hunting
They taught us how to be good hunters.

Donkey

Me, my husband and some other people were riding on a donkey to Billiluna and we camped on the way. Then we camped at the creek crossing near Billiluna and we found watermelons growing everywhere on the creek bed. We picked and ate some and took some with us.

We had two donkeys, one for swags and the other for kids to ride for fun. People having ceremony for one young boy. They came from everywhere and camped at Marapool. We had our own food, our ration from Old Mission: white flour, porridge, rice, sugar, tea and jam. After ceremony we left to go back to Old Balgo.

Nancy and Richard Tax, Malarn

Keep walking across our land

We got our rations, left and walked to Kunawarawara. We had lunch there and in the afternoon we left and camped on the way to Tjalyiwarn. We arrived there and made our camp. We stayed there for two weeks waiting for some people.

We left there and headed to Old Balgo. Camped at Kunawarawara. All the women travelling and one old man, I forgot his name. My husband was travelling self in desert with all the mens. We all had lunch at Taapayi. After lunch we left and started walking and arrived in Balgo at night.

Some people were coming from Kilang Kilang and had to travel through big Lake Gregory to Kurtu. Camped at Kurtu or Lira. Then to Kurntukuta and they killed big mob food and dingo too. Then everyone's husband came to Balgo. We gave them bush food. My husband killed dingo pup for me and I was going to eat it because I thought it was meow, you know pussycat, but I didn't eat it. I don't like eating dingo…it like eating your pet dog. So I gave it to someone.

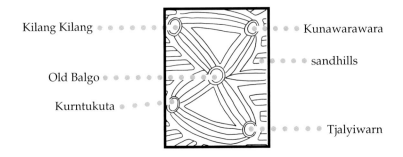

Go...come back

We went out camping, out from Old Mission to Malarn. We left our swag and went hunting for goannas. My husband went hunting for lots of goannas and then we cooked them on the fire and ate them. In the afternoon we started getting more kuka and camped halfway. We were digging for bush onions at Old Malarn.

We came back to Old Balgo and cooked more goanna near rockhole for our lunch, other side Old Mission. We got to Balgo and camped one night and got rations. Then to Tjirrtjirr this side of Old Balgo and got more goannas and bush potato. From there we went north to Lake Maddock, Yirtipuka is the blackfella name. We camped the night, killing more goanna, pussycat and getting bushtucker.

Storm came and we went to the caves and camped. In the morning we started hunting on the wet ground...we got really tired carrying swags, billycans...we never got sore feet. Then we getting seeds for damper, lukararra, warupunyu, yitakatji. We went to Mirrpi and there had lunch, more goanna.

Camped one night at the Malarn crossing and in the afternoon we went back to Old Balgo and cooked more goanna. After we got there, old people came and asked us for kuka and we gave them some. My kid was in the boys' dormitory at Old Balgo and we were travelling with Wimitji mob and his first wife, that old Nampitjin, not Yupinya, that his second wife. Yupinya had different husband then. Big mob of people. Those two Napurrulas were with us, Marri Yakuny and Nanyuma.

Feet go all the way

Me and my husband walked through the new mission before they have houses and we bin killing lots of goannas. Right up to that rockhole, Wangkaparni at the turnoff we bin go. We didn't find any water in the rockhole so we came back on the road where the rubbish tip is now. We brought lots of goannas with us and we started to smell. Had fire stick with us...no moonlight...lighting fires all the way. We camped at Tjirrtjirr.

40

People at Old Mission were looking for us and asking what time that two fella gonna come back…they thought we were lost. We cooked the goannas halfway then started going home, lighting spinifex all the way. Left our two kids behind at Old Mission, their granny bin look after them. That night we came in and everyone saw us.

Ahhh…here they are! Why you went too far? They bin ask us. *Yeah…we went too far.* We gave cooked ones to granny, Tax mother. They bin looking after our two boys.

Nancy and Richard Tax digging for yams

Morning we had more of that goanna and started out again, to Ngariyili rockhole. We got no tucker, we gotta move back to Old Mission. We went back to Old Mission and all the way we get little bit goanna and cook him up for dinner. From there we got to the mission in afternoon. We was hungry one, only had little bit of goannas. We bin camp at Old Mission that night and got rations then morningtime we went out again. We went to the creek at crossing on the way to Malarn, hunting and killing little bit goanna. Afternoon we went to Mirrpi killing more goanna…we bin camp there one night.

Morning got up and went back to Old Mission. We brought some cooked goannas back home for the kids and grandmother. We catch more halfway, goanna, roughtail, blue tongue and big frogs from the creek, well near it, the side. Lots of sheep and nanny goats we bin have at Old Mission. We got to Balgo in the afternoon and my son Ronnie said:
They coming…mum got lots of kuka.

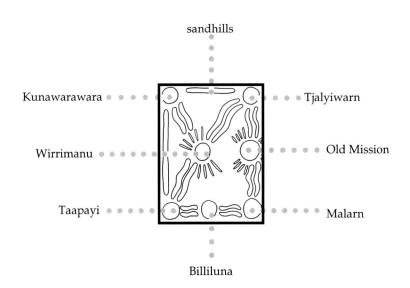

STORIES TOLD BY

Ningi Nangala

TRANSLATED BY

Tjama Napanangka

Walking, walking with no shoes

I bin walking around bush, little kid then
I bin walking everywhere, from one soakwater to another
Yinpurr, Wirntulka, living there
No mother, big mob look after us
Tjaalinu, summertime it bin start raining
Bin walking in raintime
Ngalyupi, close to Tjaalinu
Lirrwati, near Piparr, big creek there
Sometime we bin stay while
Walking around, no clothes
Making big windbreak with pinipek*
Make fire, no clothes, no blankets, no dresses
Bin sleep dry, no wet
Tjalyiwarn, no cave there only big rock hole, living water.

Sheep and nanny goats

We bin taking sheep and nanny goats to Tjalyiwarn, that place
south of Malarn. Old women bin take them nanny goats and men
take them sheep. After we take them animals, feed him grass, then
have him for dinner.

Me and other girl bin watching nanny goats, feed them that grass,
then put them in yard. Sometimes we leave them and go hunting
and come back with goanna and sand frogs. After Tjalyiwarn we go
to Kunawarawara (other side of Balgo). After go to Wirrimanu,
that Fr Macguire bin living there. From this old mission we bin
shift to new Balgo, old mission too dusty. Near the dam we bin
keeping sheep and nanny goats, fed him grass. Nothing now, finish, all bin killed. They used to feed the community.

We used to put them in the yard at night-time and sometimes go
back to Balgo and get rations on weekend. We never got any
money. Later I bin get that old money, one or two pound to buy
sugar and tea leaves. After that we bin go on holiday when we
finish work, in bush, everyone.

* spinifex

Eat him up ants

Mountain devil he like ants
We call him mingari
He bin put his tongue out for the ants
They all bin go in
That animal bin swallow them ants…he get full
Fill him up in tongue and then he swallow
He bin eating ants in one place
That animal got another two names
Tarlkayarri and minirri
Soon as he feel full he go home.

That porcupine bin get away from cave at night-time
Hunting around for them white ants
They go looking in antbed
Use his sharp long nose to get them out
Put him tongue out and them ants walk in
When he full up ants
Make that curly tongue and swallow them
That porcupine digging right round flat antbed
Finishing all them ants
Soon as he finish them ants, he go looking for more
Bin go look for another antbed
Lift them antbed with his nose and put tongue out
Ants go in
Till he get full and then he swallow.

When he finish he go home
From three antbed he bin go looking for another one
He bin make hole, let out tongue and swallow them down
Full up then
They go back home to cave
He never go in morning, he bin go night-time.
Morningtime that porcupine they get away to another cave
He go for good[*]
Sometimes he fall over when he digging hole
Might be little rock get in the way and he fall over
So he keep going…he don't like fall.

[*]all day

48

Mother different

In morningtime, man and girl…they sit down separate, and at sundown every night, he goes and meets her. This is dinnertime and they sit together. Soon it get dark, that man come to talk to woman. Sometime they find her with different father and sometime after with little baby. From that the little baby gets up and walk little bit, play around and then play with other kid from different father.

He grown up now and he have teeth, he can eat kuka. They bin find that little kid sick, he getting teeth. That kid little bigger, no more sick. Soon as pussycat bin born they walk around, sometime they sit at home and the mother go hunting around. Little puppy when he born, the mother doesn't put it in a coolamon. And soon as it grow, they walk around…mother don't look after them, he on his own.

Not like Aboriginal mother, they carry child in coolamon. Some born in bush, desert, no blanket and so mother and father make fire, make warm. The man must sit by himself, or with other man. After they take baby to father when he grows a little bit. They cut chord, not with scissors and then take it to father. They cover baby in black (ash/charcoal) and put him in smoke…that make him little bit drunk. They don't wash that black stuff off. When it would rain they make windbreak out of spinifex to keep him dry…he can't get wet…then they make a big fire.

Strange pussycat and running spinifex

At Lirrwati when we bin live there, we always went looking for bushfood. Bushtucker like carrot, potato, bin getting by digging hole in the ground. After hunting we take it back home to camp, they all happy and we cook it in the fire for dinner. Plenty bushtucker, seeds in wintertime.

This Tjampitjin from Balgo bin come and tell us mob to go to there and so we walked to soakwater at Lima. Somebody bin bring killer from Balgo to Lima. He bin cook one and we mob never seen bullock, only pussycat and kangaroo. This was the first time I eat this kuka. I bin tasting this bullock, I don't know what cat this is!
Too fat, too much rich…
I bin thinking too much this fat.

We bin stop at Kaku rockhole. What's that spinifex running around, and we all bin scared. We bin run and hide behind old people, maybe bad Dreaming spirit. Some people they bin talk and laugh at us little kids and they bin tell us that sheep not spinifex

We get to Balgo and Nanyuma tell me to camp with her and she gave me supper (in the mission). I had no clothes, I was naked. We bin living there for good in Balgo, little girl I bin come. Nanyuma bin learning English. Father bin singing out:
Come here! Poor Ningi…
Come here! That mean yanama, that Nanyuma bin tell me.

soakwater • • • • • • • • sandhills

• • • • hills

Sheep and nanny goats p. 46

Story p. 46

Gotta keep warm

I was put in a windbreak when I was little
This is really true…no lies
I bin go to Balgo as a kid
They bin put a napkin on me, like a little rag
That Father bin show us
One by one, they bin give us a rag
True, before we bin stopping in windbreak
No blanket, no clothes
Just fire, big one in wintertime
Sometimes we bin get wet mud
And put on ourself everytime it rain
Just to keep warm
No medicine in the bush
I never got sick
No coldsick
We bin use only bush medicine
We use Tjipari tree two ways
To smoke our head, or chew it to make green and put on sores
Warakatji, tie it around head or rub in head
Good for headache
We all bin born in desert
Grown up on bush medicine
That's why we bin come back to this country
In old days we used bush medicine in Balgo and rub it up.

We used to make bush shoes for summertime
Use that little tree
Put through big toe, tie around waist
Then start to thread and weave
Then put him on
Soon as we bin wearing shoes
We bin go hunting
No tobacco
But plenty of bush tobacco
That bush stuff, it's medicine
Kartiya bin give us real tobacco
We try, put in our mouth
It's right…we can have it.

Two kinds of bush tobacco
Pirnkiwarnu…found in cave
Manakarratja…found on grounds under the trees
They have white flowers
In wintertime, goanna tired and easy to find tracks
Pussycat walk around
Black snake too…
Too cold for other type of snake
It doesn't walk around.

Digging for sand frogs at Nakarra Nakarra

Two snakes

Two snakes bin travelling from Kanapilyirr
Big mob people bin dancing
It ceremony time
Them two snakes bin watching
They bin see all the womans dancing
And the grabbing of the young boys.

Kuniya
Kurnatawurn
That name of them two snake
They bin getting angry watching that dancing
They bin think
What we gotta do, eat them?
Some people bin come from another place
Bin come for that ceremony
Warlpiri, Walmajarri, Wangkajunga
Kuniyan and Warlyintjii people.

Two snakes bin eat all the people
They bin start run
Too full and eating too much people
They bin go underground
Two fella still in that claypan
Kuniya on one side
Kurnatawurn on other
In Ngukanu Palkarr, other side Piparr.

Kurnatawurn • • • • • • • • • • • • • • • • Kuniya

claypan

Soakwater

We bin living in Wartamurru soakwater in the bush
Other side of Piparr
We bin digging hole for water and we found some
And were happy
He running in waterhole
Get coolamon and drink water
Little coolamon like a cup
From Wartamurru we bin go to another waterhole, Kilkilmalu
And then to Wataparni
Bin walk around hunting at every waterhole
We bin kill big mob of animals, plenty wallabies.

Then we bin go long way to Ngarli
It summertime
Bin sitting in shade…no water
From there we bin tired from walking
He summertime you know
We bin start walking to find another shade…too hot
We bin have a dog
It bin show me where water
Dog bin go in front, he know that water
He bin wait for me, show me water, rockhole
We bin have good drink
The others bin left me behind
They bin go in front
I bin camp on my own
No water, nothing
Me slow walker
I bin cover self up in sand and leaves
Too hot
It wet under trees…mud.

Walking night-time
It suppertime, no dinner
Tired one
I bin walking…walking…walking
Dog bin find me.

He bin take me to water
Drinking…drinking…drinking
I bin get headache and vomiting
Morningtime I bin find everyone
I bin come self to camp
They all sleepy
I bin real angry
Everyone bin give me kuka to eat.

And morningtime we go looking for goanna
All bin come out to Lirrwati this side of Piparr
We bin living there and getting all the bushtucker
Tjirrilpatja, like bush carrots
Yitakatji, lukararra
All along creek bin finding tucker
Catch all them pussycat, sometime big mob goanna
Never got sick.

We bin go to some claypans, no waterhole
Lots of round things, like seeds…nyirtu
Sometime we cook it in fire and then break him up, eat him.

Ningi Nangala hunting with community women near Yaka Yaka

・・・・・・・ sandhills, Wirntulka

Bin leave my country

We gotta big waterhole in my country
Wirntulka, other side of Piparr
Only one big sandhill
We bin stopping there in living water.

It summertime we bin make sandshoes, like sandals
We go everywhere hunting around with sandals
Get pussycat, goanna, everything
I bin sit down…big girl but not woman yet
I bin kill them lizard and goanna and eat them too
We bin stop one place…too hot to walk
Afternoon he right, go hunting around.

Sometime we take him water in coolamon
Leave it in shade
Go hunting and come back and drink water
We take him home to camp, cook and eat it
You know, that wallaby
Plenty animals in bush when we bin stop there
Nothing now
No animals, that's why we bin come this way to Balgo.

We bin go to Tjaalinu and Parntjapungu
Rain start and that's the time we bin go to another place
Wet all ground
We bin find too much bush tomato
We bin get big mob, cleaning and taking seeds out.

Then put him in sun
After it nice and sweet
Put him stick through tomato for after
When it get dry we save it for later
Sometimes cook it in fire to hotten him
It dry and we put in coolamon
Squash him, put in water and take him out
It like ice-cream…true, nice and sweet.

From there we bin go to Parntatja
All bin living there in sandhill
We bin get plenty wood
No blanket, we bin have…nothing.

Rain bin wetten ground
Bin put plenty fire in sandhill
Living there
We bin get mud and put on us…no blanket, nothing
That mud make us warm.

After rain, soon as rain bin finish…all gone rain
We walk around for hunting
After we talk:
All gone rain, we'll make him plenty fire
Get little bit warm, get dry
Raining time, we take big firestick to another place…
No matches
We bin find big log and we bin light him
It to keep us safe
We got fire for after
Go hunting around killing all the animals
Go back home, cook and eat it.
Sometime other people coming
They come and find fire, big log fire
They really happy.

Kungkala, that little stick to light him up fire
Men bin get long stick and little one
They bin rub that little stick up and down to get fire

All bin come this way to Balgo
Someone bin talk:
No one in bush, they all gone to mission
That's why we bin come.

We bin see tracks on the way
People know that he not bullock…he cheeky one
Some they know it buffalo
When you see them tracks you gotta light big fire
He gotta go long way
That fire frighten him.

Tjarralaparlparl – pigeon

He walk around camp eating something, grass, porridge, rice
Anything people bin throw away
He talk like:
Hhmm, hhmm, hhmm…

In Dreamtime
When people go hunting they listen
Someone singing out
People think it other people
Someone bin say:
No, it that pigeon
He got red eye, he sharp one on head
Bin get that in Dreamtime
Carrying that coolamon of water on his head.

Yaka Yaka, now
He bin walking around eating rubbish, anything
All the kids frighten him
Sometimes them kids get shanghai and shoot it
Cook it and eat it for supper.

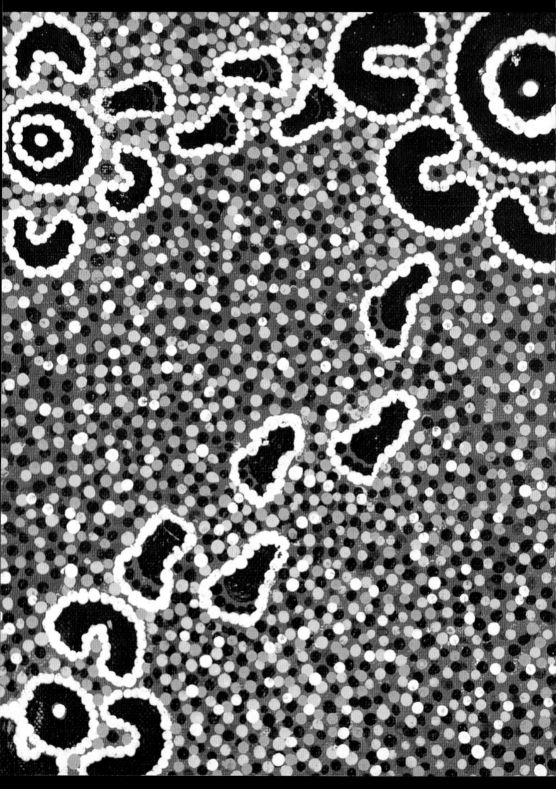

Shifting all the way

In Tjalyiwarn they bin have a mud house
We bin living there
Then we bin go to Tjumurnturr
Bin working carting posts and antbed[*] on donkey
Bin make house...Mosquito too.

From there we all bin shift to Old Balgo
All bin living there building houses, school
One truck for loading food we bin have in Old Balgo
Everyone bin living there now for good
Policeman come around to pick up the men
Bin take them to Halls Creek in jail
They bin walking all the way, no mutika, just horses
Some taken for killing sheep.

Priest one bin say we all gotta leave this Balgo
Too much dust...no water too
Gotta shift to Wirrimanu
People first bin shift to Taapayi
We all bin waiting for them houses to finish
Father bin take rations to the people every Saturday
We bin have plenty karnti, bush potatoes in Taapayi.

You fella gotta wait till them houses finish
They bin build convent, dormitory and shop
All the people bin building houses
Young people that time but they really old now
Sunfly, Payi Payi husband
That Mick Gill, Putja Putja husband
They all old men now
Soon as the house get up
People bin come from everywhere.

First time people from Billiluna and Sturt Creek bin come
We all bin shift from Taapayi to Wirrimanu
Kukatja people bin building all the way

[*]Antbed used for flooring material

Everyone bin say: *We wanna go to Wirrimanu*
Only Kukatja people bin building, not Walmajarri
Kukatja people bin build that homestead too, Ngalyupi
All the pensioners today, when they young
They bin build Wirrimanu.

Some young boys from Wirrimanu all grown up here
They bin go mustering in the stock camp in Ngalyupi
Patricia Milner husband bin working at that stock camp
That Jimmy Tjuka bin stop at school in Wirrimanu
After school finish he bin ride horses in Ngalyupi
My mob bin feed him bushtucker
Walmajarri people never grow up here
Kukatja mob bin grow that Jimmy up, give him bushtucker
He bin grow up Kukatja.

See painting p.62

STORIES TOLD BY

Ngunytja Napanangka Mosquito

TRANSLATED BY

Patricia Lee, Rhonda Tax
Nancy Kungkulu Tax
Tjama Napanangka

Who got more meat?

Our mothers use to tell us to go eat munyurn and go out for tjalapa, little skink lizard. We and the others would go out hunting for yanpakarratja…he quiet snake. We used to get that munyurn but I never eat it, reckon it different taste from other plum bushes. I not happy enough to eat it, burn it in fire and start grinding it. Looks like sandalwood. We go back to camp and play around next to this rockhole. All the big people use to go into the waterhole to get water and give to the kids…they happy for that water.

When I was kid we used to hide behind spinifex and see who got more meat out hunting and run to them. It big shame to count, some bin tell us. After go and see how many your mother or granny bring home. When I was a kid we used to grind that munyurn, make a big mess on the grinding stone and leave it. Other kids bin tell our mothers. Sometime our granny used to take us hunting for munyurn and we used to get lots then go sit back under the tree. When we used to grind that bushtucker, we used to rub hair with the juice to make it long.

When the kids' stay back at camp we never fight, we always good friends. We work hard at that grinding and never swear. We used to be really good. They smoke us so we don't swear. We never used kartiya words…never told kids they were rubbish.

That other kids' mothers come back from hunting.
We ask: *How many goannas your mother bring back?*
Kids hungry and they want to know when goannas come. Mother go back and get the cooked ones to feed everyone. We bin talking about goannas. When mother gave us goanna we happy for that and when someone get the smallest one he start cry. Mother bin ask why he cry and she tell him to just eat it. We rub our face with the goanna fat to make it shiny after we finish eating.

After we use to eat munyurn we go out and look for another type of food called yirrakampa in another rockhole. That yirrakampa really nice, it look like sugar. Everytime the women go in front to get goanna, all the way the kids go behind to see how many they get. They find rockhole and we stay there…he got plenty of food. If there no food they go to different one.

When that wife one go hunting and see if that fruit ready…and she go back home to tell husband. But they not ready, they still raw. They go and visit all the time and wait for it to get cooked*. The kids used to go eat this tucker but it really kangaroo food and the kids used to steal it. When they go back to camp their mother tell them they all gonna go looking out for food.
You kids gotta stay here…plenty of that kangaroo food…you gotta make fire and eat him.

We kids used to light fire on spinifex and that fire burnt that grass-hopper. We bin eat them too. We used to run back to camp and tell the old people, who don't go out hunting, that there a lot of that bushtucker yirrakampa. Then they come back and that fruit always fall. Leaves look like lemon leaves and the fruit looks like plums. Sometime woman shake it and they start to fall, and collect them and take them home. Person who cleans it has to collect it and it for them.

Some kids they rude, they don't deserve it, so they get fruit away from tree, not straight under it. That woman has to share fruit with other kids, not just own ones, even if they got runny nose.

One day they eat too much and stomach get too big, too fat, too much full…eat, eat, eat. When they eat too much they can't move. Not only husband and wife get tucker, everyone and they share it with all the kids, even if their mother and father are out hunting.

Old woman go hunting and that yirrakampa, they get cooked: he ripe. They get coolamon and go get it. They break him and put in sun to dry. They do it gently, they don't talk to make noise. If you do, and come back next day, they still raw.

You can't make noise and he ready next day. We tiptoe back to see if it cooked. It special fruit. If we make noise it still raw. If you really want that mangarri you walk away slowly and come back later and he cooked. When we heat that yirrakampa and eat it, we get sore mouth so we put leaf on to make it better. I like this one, not that munyurn.

*Ripe

Girl eats like mouse

Mother bin have one daughter
Bin get him bushtucker and something like grass
They put it in coolamon
Take it back to camp, make big damper
Grinding it into the dough and cook it.

The daughter won't eat pussycat, goanna, anything
Only likes bushtucker
She like yanpurrtju
Spinifex hopping mouse
She no marry anyone.

From nowhere, man bin come out
He bin keep away, sit down and watch
Can't talk to woman
Daughter bin talk
Give him something…tucker
Mother one bin say
I'm not relation for that man, he not my cousin…
They can get lost.

Mother and daughter bin go hunting separate
That man bin come out
Girl had big milk
He grab her, he bin love that young girl
Mother go back self to camp
Man bin take that daughter one
They married
Daughter got witjirrki, that wild fig
She bin give it to mother back at the camp
That man get big mob of animals
Little wallaby, bandicoot, to give to mother.

I don't want it, you can take it back…
That mother don't like that man
She bin talk rude way
Telling off that man for giving meat.

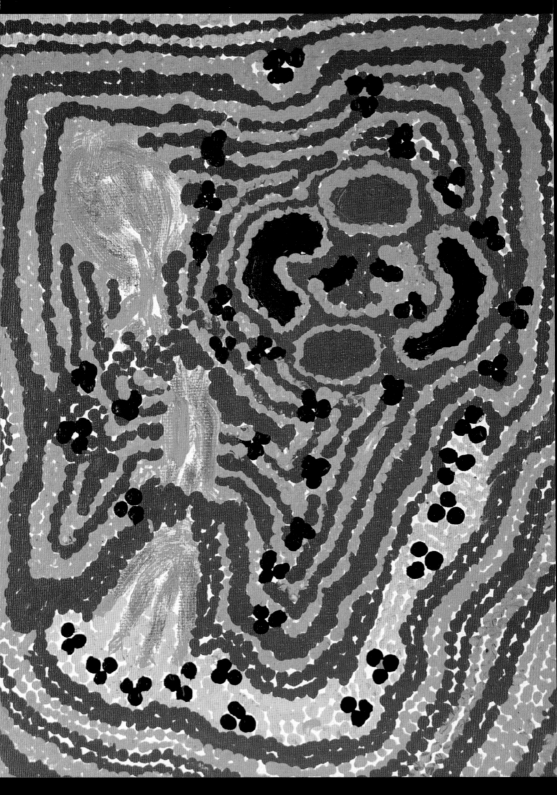

See key p.72

Night-time when the mother sleeping
Man bin talking…talking…talking
He bin get angry at mother of that girl.

Morningtime, before sunrise
Mother bin go getting bushtucker
Gathering…gathering…gathering
Bushtucker from a tree that the wind bin pull to the ground
Mother bin putting all the bushtucker in coolamon
Ready to cook
She bin talking:

Kurlarnpararra minyinpararra ngalkurla ngalya lirrkati tjaaku
Kurlarnpararra minyinpararra
Ngurrpa, ngurrpa

That man, he watching which way they talking and singing
He bin throw big rock
Woman bin screaming:
Paaaaaaaaaaaa
Story gonna be haunting you…
Mother one that mouse, she dead, finish.

Man bin marry that girl
He bin teach that girl to eat meat.

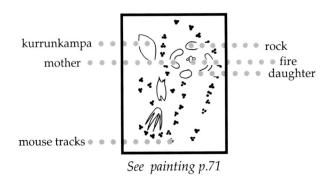

See painting p.71

Kakarratuly – red mole

Somewhere west in soakwater named Tipurnpa
In Dreamtime, one kakarratuly had two babies
That animal was living underground and gave birth there
Didn't have nyupa...that mean boyfriend
She had two beautiful kids in my country somewhere
They bin stay underground in the tunnels
Mother one bin show them kids the hole to see outside.

She went outside to get food and take them for a walk
She bin check if anyone outside first
They eat white ants in big hollow log
After eating they bin full up
They bin go back to hole, inside to keep warm
Shut entrance, cover it all over
That way no snakes can get in and eat them
That country name is Maanypa.

Men and womans bin come to that place
For dancing ceremony
That mother one start singing:

Pantururri yirririlu wananu
Pantururri pantururri
Purr, purr, purr

That Kakarratuly bin learning song and dancing from people
After all that singing they bin go inside hole
Morning get up, and eat them white ants.

Mother use to sing songs for those two little ones
And use to eat ants after singing
Clapping hands
Purr...purr...purr.

One dog came across and heard them singing
He wanted to eat them
Dog was digging and digging hole, trying to find them
He can smell them and he getting anxious about them
The three still underground hiding.

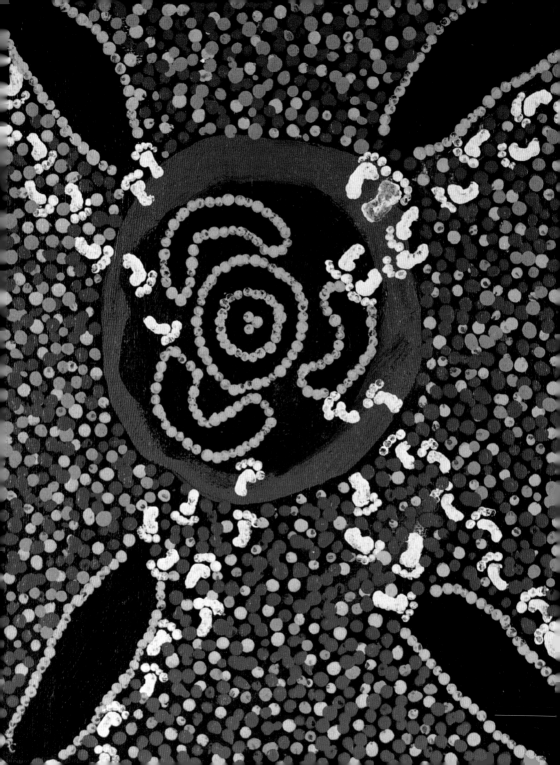

That dog was looking for them and couldn't find them
But he went to sleep right on the hole that animal covered up
When the dog was asleep
That kakarratuly start digging another tunnel
Quiet, quiet they run away
Mother went back to stay right under the sleeping dog, to trick him.

She started making lot of noise to cover up the two babies
Dog thought there were three
But the little two were safe in another tunnel.

That dog still smell them two little ones
He started walking and put his foot right the hole and ate one
Looking around for the other one
He found the other one and ate it too…
He not far from the first
The two little ones taste like sand
He was feeling a bit sick and vomited right there
After that he went to camp, travelling on empty gut.

That big dog was travelling from my country
Around Walkarli, Piparr
He telling each group what tribe they gotta be
You gotta be Kukatja
You gotta be Wangkajunga
After he went east, Warlpiri side, to join all the other dogs
Only the mother kakarratuly was alive and still there
She went underground.

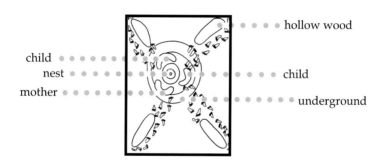

I understand

When we grown up we understand everything. We go walking around for bushtucker called pampilanytji. It green beans. All the mothers told us not to fight when we stay in camp, just to sit there.

When we go hunting we go on top sand dune to look around for tucker, find tree and go and get him. This time it end of wintertime, September, and we get plenty pampilanytji, it ready. When we used to get it, that bean we put under coals if they not ripe. If they ripe we just eat them. Today maybe that bean still there around that sand dune area. You don't eat the skin, just the inside, clean…clean… open it and eat inside. We used to run back to camp and tell the old people who don't go out hunting that there a lot of bushtucker.

When we used to finish hunting that bushtucker, go back home and play hide and seek. Kawarli…kawarli, that mean hurry up, run and hide. Turn around and look.
You out, I can see you
These days when they play ball they say
Kulila kulila
Which mean look around.

All the old woman sit in the windbreak, they look all dusty, ash all round and hair not comb, all their hair curly. Use to get spinifex, not real one, it like a branch and they burn it and put through hair. Burn (charcoal) that hair and then grease him up.

Womans use to go hunting looking for bushtucker to bring back home. When I was little I lost my mother. My granny grew me up. Antbed Tjungurrayi mother bin grow me up. Next day we showed big people where we find that bean bushtucker. We all help the old womans…true…no lies. Throw him in fire and cook it. Some old womans follow us, we not go far and we carried her coolamon, stick, and helped her get that bean. They finish in cold-time.

Those kids, when they three or four, no drink breast milk of mother, they used to eat bushtucker. Our faces and body used to be real dirty. Other mothers used to feed anyone, not just her kids.

When smallest kid didn't have teeth, other kids would bite the food and make it soft for them to eat. Even for my aunty we used to bite that food and give it to her…she had no teeth.

Mother and father come back from hunting and we were waiting for all the stuff. Grandmothers stay in windbreak looking after us. We would play not far from them. We not only used to live at one living water but go to another one to fetch food. We went to different soakwater and joined another mob, family and all the kids happy.

Families hunting

This story when I was kid.

They went hunting, killing all the goannas, chasing kuka and following the tracks. We follow the lizard — killing them in the hole. I got no mother…aunty or stepmother look after us. They come back home, make a fire and cook them lizards. When that skin gets cooked on the fire, we dig a hole next to the fire and cover all them lizards up and leave them to cook.

We make the ground oven and wait till they get cooked. Dig them up then we eat that tail part first and we give that tjira (oil-fat) to our friends and kids to share out. We rub the fat on our skin and chew the tail and neck up. We eat them one by one and chuck the head part out, he rubbish. We go back home for water, we really thirsty. On the way to home we track more.
Mine, mine that one, I'll kill 'em…over there, tracks, fresh ones.

Walk separate and spread out, little bit long way.
Kuka, we shout.
The lizard gets frightened and gets in the hole. We get them on the way to home and cook them in the camp for supper. Our grandmother and grandfather come back for us with a big mob kuka and they make a fire near the camp. They used to leave all the old people and kids in camp and we never fight, just playing around. We look around for our mothers, waiting for them to come back from hunting.

The kids ask, and then we see them coming from long way. The women first with orange lizards. They bring the coolamons with big mob animals. We watch them coming over the sandhills as they come closer to the camp. They come with coolamon and the kids check the coolamons to see how much kuka they bring. Bin bring lots of goannas, lizards and my grandmother's got lots of meat. We get happy.

Everybody drink some water and start cooking the lizards. He get up from hole when it's hot-time, and womans look around and find them. She come with her coolamon, sits down and has a rest.

She tells us to get wood and give it to the grandmothers. We good kids and we get that wood. I'm thinking if I'm gonna get big piece of meat.

Nungurrayi, my grandmother, bin light a fire and clean that lizard up, cook it in the fire and put it in the side near the fire. We didn't eat bullock meat, only wallaby, rat kangaroo, black nose snake, that was our meat. That keep us healthy and alive. Our grandfathers and aunties would kill all the kuka for us and our uncles would put them in the fire oven and cover them in hot coals or hot sand. Start having a rest when we cook it, big rest from hunting… everyone tired. Then we get happy and wait for the meat. We play around, rolling, rolling in the sand. Sometimes when we have to wait long time, we get him tears.

Our grandmother gets the kuka out from the fire and moves the hot fire away with a stick. Then she lifts up the kuka with a stick and takes the goanna out and cleans it with the hot coals. She gives the small kids two and we share it around, one, two, three each. Grandmother clutches the stone and smashes the bones on the rock.

When the kids finish eating the kuka, the bones go to the grandmother and she smashes it. We go travelling around from place to place and gives it to the people to share it out with the kids. They eat the meat and shift to another place, another soakwater. We'll go back to the same place and the old people bin shout out to the kids:
Don't go fast, walk slowly, stay close.

Mothers and fathers go in front, hunting and killing all the way…they dig for water with little coolamons, right down till water comes up. That mud comes close and start get wet ground. They get some spinifex and put some down and get some water. That water comes up and we get some water with coolamon. Grandmother gets up and put the goanna outside the waterhole, goes down and has a drink. She then goes back and put the coolamon down in the shade and goes and get some more wood for goanna.

Go around, collect some more leaves and wood, break it up and make a fire with a firestick, no matches then, only firestick. She lights the spinifex all the way and takes that firestick everywhere. When the fire gets finished they get kungkala, that mean firestick, and make another fire.

Put some yipiri (spinifex) under the kungkala and hold with their foot. Old mans puts string (wood string) and makes a hole and starts rubbing on the wood. Then he takes the strap and ties it up and puts the kungkala round his waist to make a fire when the stick finishes.

Husband and wife go out hunting and we stay in the camp. All the kids wait for them and go for a little walk to get some water and then go back. They go sit down near the fire…those kids, they all mad ones!
Ahh! They left some meat for us, this one's mine and that one's yours — don't cry for it!

Some kids don't share that food and they get too full so they gotta sleep, have a rest.
Ah, they coming from hunting with lots of goanna.
That mob happy we kids still alive. They tell the kids to get them water and the kids go because they see lots of goanna and latju on the coolamon, plenty there. Kids gets really happy and works for grandmother and grandfather or aunty and uncle real quick. So they get big feed.

They run and get some water, they really hungry for goanna. That grandmother gets the cooked meat and put it down on the ground ready. Those kids yell out:
Hurry up and cook the meat — I'm hungry.
That grandmother bin tell them to wait and not be greedy:
Everyone will get some. You'll be hunting for goanna when you get big. When that mountain devil get big he know which one to hunt for…he didn't miss going out hunting. He teaches that little one to kill own kuka. You gotta learn too. Grandmother she mash the bones and put them in the coolamon and when he get full put some left over for next time.

We were healthy and little bit fat, not skinny one. We never do washing, no showers in the bush, little kids always dusty ones. In raintime we bin doing lot of swimming in flooded spinifex…up and down, camp to water. Grandparents use to sleep in front of the fire and the kids behind, that husband sleep other side. It cold-time and they get bush honey for kids when they go sleep. They soaked that pukara in the water and the little kids suck it.

Nungurrayi, Ngunytja and John Mosquito

We camping out three or four days then shift to another place. All the kids they get happy for that honey, it like sugar. Night-time another honey, shake the honey on the coolamon and start gathering them bush sugar in the desert. When the sun comes up, no more sugar. We bring up the sugar and put it in the coolamon and take it back to the old ladies. The kids help their mothers for eating that sugar and to cook it.

Nunpi is like a little wallaby, he goes up and down blocking holes with sand. He buries himself under the ground and follows them tracks. He puts weights on them and kills them with his foot…on the outsides, then inside. Man follows them tracks and gets in the hole…they're over there.
Ahh, he's gone back, go and look that side — look inside the log for wayurta, he little possum.

He climbs up with axe in bag and he spears him, kills it and throws it down to the ground. He gets happy for that big mob of kuka. Used to go out hunting ourselves, killing blue tongues own way, and when we were getting big mob we take it back to the camp.

He get some hair from the tail of that wallaby — it white one from that wayurta, nunpi and pintitiri — to put in the beard of old man. He take some for his wife to put in the hair, behind or in front, to make hair come down, make it long. They put some in the kids hair, it looks nice and long. They never had clothes. That's the right way, like kartiya use ribbons, make them pony tail…are you listening? It make his kid look nice.

Husband go out hunting to get some more and takes it to his wife to cook. When that animal gets cooked, them white people chuck the bone out when they finished eating the meat. We do this time now, but desert people used to smash it on the stone…bone and all they bin having, giving it out to the kids. Wife one he tell them fat little kids to get one from her grandmother. I was sulking for kuka when granny bin give them out to other kids because she should give me more. I used to sit back way, facing back to grandmother and crying, me spoilt one.

My grandmother passed away in Tangku this side of Christmas Creek. Another grandmother is Walmajarri, another one Kukatja side. Kukatja mob were listening to Walmajarri people and how they were speaking. Walmajarri mob came from another place, and that kartiya can't understand Kukatja or Walmajarri. We bin understand straight away. Anyway we camp one night, then start going to another place.

We bin see big fire, somebody lighting him. That fire long way, it like sign, so we get up and start walking and camp half way. Afternoon we bin coming in. Another person got up and and saw people coming from another place, another tribe. They recognised them, they got no clothes and they cry to them. They people coming from long way…desert people and they were listening to each other talking. They were giving out some meat to those people who were coming in from another place. They bin give them boomerang, spear, woomera too.

Getting closer to time to pick kamitji, he ready, really ripe and everybody came in, getting that juice from the berries. We didn't eat it when we was kids, only mothers, aunties and mother-in-law. They sit down and finish that kamitji then go back another place.

They bin go round and eat that bushtucker tjatupitji…chew it up like tobacco and put it in side of the ear. They getting black tongues and mouths from that tjatupitji. Even them kids run round and collect them and eat it too.

When that kamitji plant gets ready, we get long stick and put it in the stick and take it back home. We don't share it to their mothers, just eat it ourselves. We didn't know how to cook it on the fire, only the old people know and they chew and throw it away when it has no taste…so we have another one…chew some more, then we go to sleep. Old people come and make sure we all sleeping and none missing.

The kids get dry skins from sleeping near the fire, got no clothes, no comb. Kids got plenty of kuka when grandmother and grandfather got big mob meat. Some kids say that he gonna hit us but when he sits down we run to grandparents. They bin ask us to get water and we get the coolamon and run for the water so we get the first goanna.

When he drinks the water he puts the beard in the water too. Kids go get some wood when that old man says and they break the woods and put it together to make a fire. Old man takes the guts out from the goanna and share the meat with the kids.

Ngularn is bushtucker that starts falling off from the tree. He sugar, sweet honey, like sugar heaped up on the ground when they gathering it. Kaliny kaliny is same like honey but you gotta suck them. They save some of that honey in their string bag for next time. Kurrkarpi, he like another sugar that we use to make tea with living water, yinta. Pukara, kaliny kaliny and ngularn, they all like a sugar and we bin find them in desert and put it in the sun to dry. Then we come back and break them and put in big coolamon.

Piparr country…other side of Piparr, I was learning. We were all gathering up the families and relations; Nangala, Nungurrayi, Napanangka…Wimitji's families, travelling around cold weather time. I forgot about my family, I was little girl. I thought I had no family and when I got big, husband took me away. Husband took me to another place, to his mob, Kukatja mob. That my first husband.

Ngunytja and John Mosquito

Women's business

Father bin give his daughter to son-in-law. Other man just can't come in and get wife, got to be right skin. Mother don't talk to that boy, he stay away, they don't sit together. That son-in-law gotta be good hunter, he give his wife meat and she give it to her mother and father. When they used to get lots of food they put it in hole and cover with coolamon and get it next day.

Mother and father used to keep that girl at another soakwater. Send someone to get the man from different soakwater to tell him that she ready to be married. You gotta wait for the right one.

Maybe about six months she ready to have baby, not for anybody but for that right boy. When the woman pregnant, she only eat bandicoot, no emu. If they eat other things they might get sick. When she pregnant in bush she only drink water in daytime not night-time. Don't give your daughter to somebody in another community or different group. You gotta give her to someone in your group.

That girl can easy feel baby moving in stomach…he might be ready. She keep it secret. She not allowed to tell husband about baby or when he gonna come. That girl has it in a windbreak and grandmother or sister help out, not mother or aunty…big shame if they do. They can only see it when he out. Three or four weeks she stay out there then goes to father. Not like white people…them women ready to have baby and the husband there waiting. Baby comes out and starts crying:
Nga…nga…nga.
That father or husband can't ask if it boy or girl. It sacred, he don't have to know…not allowed to ask.

The woman rests and sister or granny bring water, like a servant. When baby born, mother can't feed him for one or two days, she nurses it till the breasts get full. After that they get special leaves to smoke baby to get it strong again.

Now young girls come back from Derby[*] and husband sees it before baby is smoked. Baby gotta be smoked first. When I was little, I was company for that girl but I don't stare, I look other way. I'd bring

[*]Town where the main hospital for the Kimberley region is located

water. I used to work. That mother gets smoked and she stay lying down till pain settle down.

Wife one she weak after baby, that husband go hunting for food getting more kuka and water. He give it to grandmother to give to his wife…she still out there. When that husband get away, go hunting, the wife can go get water in rockhole. She can't see him, she might get sick.

Girl stays there till that baby belly button falls off and does toilet which old woman put all over it. Then he ready to go to husband. Get black stuff from burnt stick and put on forehead and chest of baby so he don't hiccup.

They live together that husband and wife till their baby turn around self. Then they go out hunting and take baby along to another soakwater to find grandparents. Before they come to the soakwater, they light fire and the father-in-law knows that they are coming.

They know the smoke, like a signal. If they see tree and green grass and birds flying away that mean there's a soakwater ahead…butterflies too.

The grandparents see how strong and big he is and they very happy for that child. That husband gotta go all the way hunting for food to give to his father- and mother-in-law. That make them very happy.

After, when the baby gets bigger, the parents dig a hole in the sand and he sits in there, doesn't make humbug. Getting big, he ready to start crawling then walking. When she takes baby for hunting, put it on shoulders like a kangaroo so she can use coolamon for kuka. When they smoke babies and when baby make toilet they rub all over. That's why he don't cry or get spoilt…he let his mother work.

That feeling

Long time ago
Old man had them feelings in his foot
Kartapila
It means someone coming
He bin watching out that old man
And went up the hill to light fire
It was true, this man bin coming from other place
Come to visit
He brought meat for the people
They all talking together
When he bin giv'em food, he start crying
They had a sorry meeting*.

*Mourning

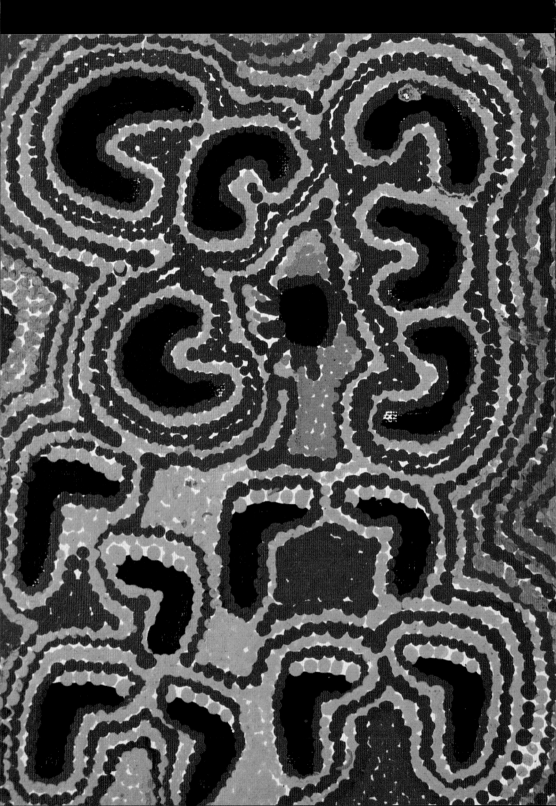

After meeting he was talking all day
Law time stories…
Other people sitting down bin bring him wood
They bin make windbreak
Then everyone went to sleep.

When he got up from sleep
He got his spear and gave it to his mate
It's a present, from long way away
He keep going to another soakwater
Someone light him fire
He doesn't tell people where he going
Stay two or three days then leaves to another soakwater.

The old man, he bin get more feeling in toe
His son coming this time from long way
He hears things like big telephone
Hears big mob of people talking from long way
His son bin come too…true!

People get a feeling in their heart, kurtutu
Pumping…pumping…pumping
Feel that blood moving
That mean that you gotta go searching
Go looking for people who have them feelings in foot.

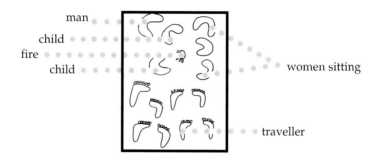

STORIES TOLD BY

Nyangayi Napangarti

TRANSLATED BY

Tjama Napanangka

Willy Wagtail

Big ceremony time, in Dreamtime. They bin grab little boys and they give him present. Willy Wagtail bin ask:
What about me?
This old man says: *Nothing, we can't give you presents.*
He bin sit down quiet and watch everyone give other boys parcels. But nothing to him. Willy Wagtail got no family.

Old man go up to boy sitting near Wagtail.
Nothing for you, Wagtail.
Boys got hairbelt, boomerangs, headbands. Night-time they bin having ceremony. Morningtime, old people bin give boys presents but not Wagtail.
Not you, only other boys. You got no family.
He bin watching them presents go to other boys.

That Wagtail bin get up and putting hand out:
Me…for me?
Nothing. Every morning, same thing. They bin pass presents straight over him. There big mob people sitting around and Wagtail in the middle. He bin putting hand out — nothing.

That Willy Wagtail bin singing:
What I gotta do? Go see my cousin brother, I got no family here.
His sister bin tell him to go long way from people. He had only one sister. Only two wagtail, brother and sister.
I keep going to lake…sit long way.

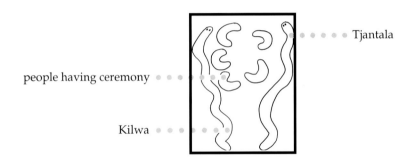

That Wagtail went to lake to tell the water snakes, his cousins:
I got nothing, I got no family there, they never give me anything…no spear, hairbelt…nothing.
Them two water snakes, Kilwa and Tjantala bin get up. They bin tell that Wagtail: *We go sit down quiet.*

Them people still having ceremony and sister bin sit long way from people. That Willy Wagtail bin tell him two snakes to stop and watch ceremony.

Kilwa and Tjantala bin go right round the people…long way. They bin make little cloud, raining little bit. Big rain, too much. People in ceremony bin say: *He raining now…he big rain.*
Night-time that water bin wash away everything, all the people bin drowning. Only brother and sister bin alive, all the others finish. They never give that Wagtail anything.

Two snakes went back to the Lake, making toilet on the way, too full from eating people. We gotta lake at place called Kilwa and another one at place called Tjantala, after them two Dreaming snakes. They living there, underground. They still there.

Two cockies

White Cocky bin get good bushtucker
Red Cocky bin get rubbish bushtucker
White one come back from hunting
Bin cook them bush carrots and give to daughters
Red one bin give daughters rubbish food
Sit down at separate camps
White Cocky go one way for hunting
Red one go different way
Mothers went out hunting.

Kids bin come together to play
White Cocky kids bin give red ones some mangarri
Red one taste it…he good one
That red one bin talk:
You fella get good tucker
You lucky one

We gonna show our mother this food
We bin eating rubbish food.

Little red Cocky bin give that food to mother
You taste it, you try him
Wara — really nice
Morningtime red Cocky bin watching
Which way I gotta go?
I gotta follow that girl.

Red Cocky bin follow that white one
Oh! From here
She bin getting good food
White Cocky bin get up
What you bin following me for?
Ahhh…you never tell me you get good tucker
You bin come this way every morning.
White one get up
Two fella bin fight
They bin keep fighting
That white one really greedy
Who gonna win?
All the kids in camp, left behind.

White Cocky bin win
Not much blood
Red one get too much blood
Couldn't walk, two of them
Two fella bin crawl into that cave
Other side of Tjantala
Lurrpungutjangka, name of that cave.

Now he sit down in tree
Can't walk
Too weak from that fight.

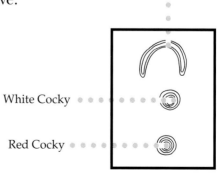

See painting p.96

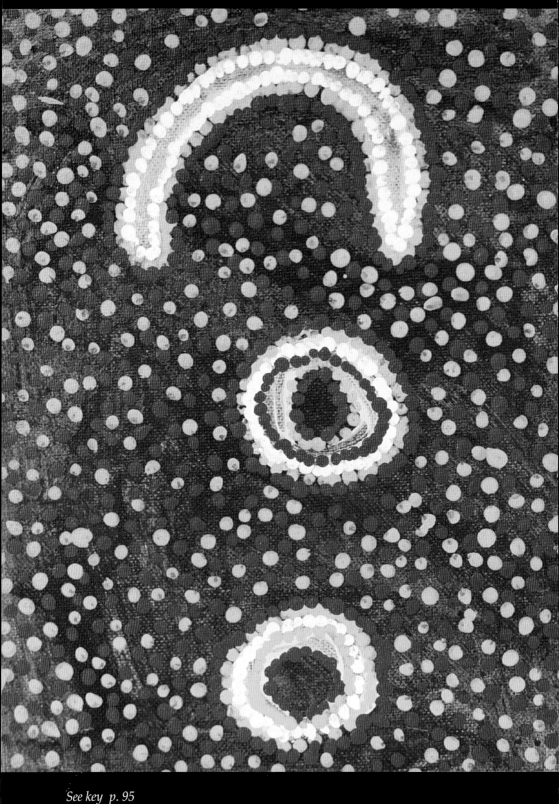

See key p. 95

The fire chucker

That old man bin growing up his grandchild near Kupartiya. That kid not little one. It wintertime and raining and they making big windbreak to put big fire.

Where I gotta sleep, grandpa?
That old man bin tell him to go far, not near fire. That kid bin say he too cold, want to sleep near fire. That old man bin tell him to sleep in corner, he might get into trouble. That old man bin tell lies. That old man bin get wet ground and rub kid in mud.
You mud bird.
It punishment. That man not sorry for that little boy. He shaking all the way, too cold.
Come on grandpa, I wanna sleep near fire.
That man bin tell him that he get in trouble. He bin tell that kid:
You gotta be rain maker, you can't have warm place.

Morningtime, little boy go hunting, grandpa too weak. Kid bin get big mob animals, goanna, pussycat to give to old man.
Can I sit down near fire, I'm shaking? No, your mother might get into trouble.
He bin tell that boy lies. Old man bin get wet ground and rub mud into that kid skin, but it all wet. He shaking even more.

Everytime he bring animals, he give to old man. That old man bin tell him the food too hot and he gotta wait to get cool.
Can I sit near fire?
No, your mother might get sick. Don't break the Law.
He bin sleep in cold place under spinifex, shaking.

Kid bin go hunting, getting wallaby, pussycat, anything. He bring and give it to old man. Night-time, old man bin go to toilet. That little boy bin get up from sleep and getting firestick and chuck him long way. Old man bin frightened. He run and wake up that boy. Little boy…he clever one.
You bin see that big light, like star? That old man bin say.
Boy bin say he sleep. He bin get that boy up to look for something.
Nothing…might be big star.
That boy bin tricking him…they bin go back to sleep.

Morningtime that little boy went out hunting and looking for that firestick. He bin find it and keep going. That old man never bin give him fire. Old man bin waiting…waiting…when he gonna come back? That kid clever one, he keep going.

Sun go down and that little boy never come back. Old man bin sing out for that little boy. Bird bin answer: *Uuuuuuuu.*
Grandpa think he went long way, but that bird bin tricking him. He think that bird him grandson. *Ahh my grandson, he close.*

Old man sleep, thinking about boy, might be something happen.
Morningtime I gotta go look for that boy.
That boy not worry about grandfather, he keep going.
Morningtime, he bin get up, following little boy track.
Ahhhhh …that boy bin throw firestick, he bin tricking me. I gotta go back and get everything, my spear, boomerang, nulla nulla.
That grandfather really angry, he wild.
Morningtime he keep following that kid. Boy bin making big fire and windbreak and cooking big mob of animals. That old man bin see smoke coming slow all the way. He bin get closer to that camp…closer…closer…and spear it. But nothing, that kid already gone.

Young boy keep going, camp one night, cooking food and leaving some behind for grandfather and keep going. Old man bin come, follow track:
Maybe he here?
He bin find wallaby and eat it. No kid.
Old fella keep chasing that young kid.

Old man bin come to water. Little boy on other side bin tell him to come through but that water bin pull old man in. He bin run out.
Old Man bin worried:
Too deep, I can't cross over. What I gotta do my grandson?
Kid bin say: *That water not deep, he shallow one.*
Old man bin put spear in water: *He deep one, come and get me.*
That kid bin tell him: *No. I bin come through there.*

Young boy bin say he got wallaby. He bin chuck him and old man opened his mouth. Hot stone covered in fat. Old man bin scratching chest…it too hot for him.

Something you bin give me. Hot stone you bin chuck me.
That man, he scratch himself and he bin go up a tree…he bin change into a possum and bin stop there for good. Snake bin grab that boy again and take him to mother and family. Water snake rub that boy in red ochre and put hair belt on and all bin dancing… mother, aunty and sisters. Snake bin grow up that boy now. Everyone bin dancing for that boy. Mother and father bin crying for that boy, they all happy. He man now that boy.

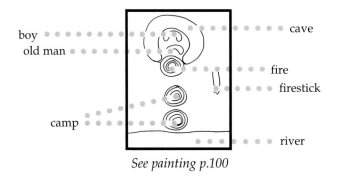

See painting p.100

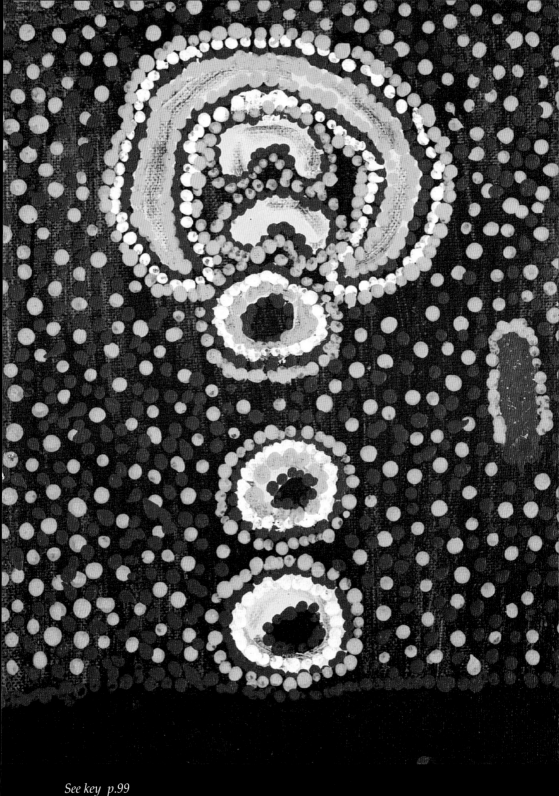

See key p.99

That other Yunpu

Long time ago that other Yunpu, husband and wife bin living
there. They old ones and greedy. Morningtime, early, they bin look
that way…west. Someone coming, and that old man bin run to
cave, waiting. That two young boys bin look, they bin travelling
long way and that old woman bin make coldsick damper, blow him
nose in that damper. Not really true damper.

Old woman crying for two boys, but she greedy one. Old woman
give damper to that two boys and they bin break it and eat it after
that old woman bin finish crying. After they eat it, old woman bin
say she wanna show the animal inside cave, lungkarr, he like a
wallaby. Old woman bin tell them boys:
Me weak, you go inside, that animal not far.

Soon as them boys bin go inside, that old man kill him two fellas
with a stick. He bin kill them in nose. Old woman waiting outside.
They bin take them home, cook it and eat it all night. After that, in
morningtime, they bin watching the road and they see two more
people coming up. Old woman bin tell that old man to run inside
that cave. She blow coldsick in damper ready for the two young
boys. Woman bin crying:
I'm your granny.
But not really, they strangers. She bin give them damper and they
bin eat it.
*I can't go hunting, I'm weak. I'll take you to that lungkarr in cave. You
gotta catch him for me.*

That old woman bin take them to cave, not far, that animal there.
Them two men get in cave to get that lungkarr…finish. Old man
bin kill them with stick. Old man chuck them out and woman bin
pull them. Old woman bin take one and old man other one to
camp, make fire, cut him up, cook and eat it all night waiting for
another mob to come.

Morningtime they get up and look, two more coming. Old man bin
run to that cave and the woman start making coldsick damper and
crying for those grandson. Old woman bring it and give to boys
and they eat it and she tell them that she too weak to go hunting.

I'll take you to that lungkarr, me too weak to hunt…it not far…you gotta go inside and get that animal.

Them two young fella go inside cave and soon as they bin get inside that old man bin kill him. He chuck them outside, take him home, cook it and eat it all night. Morningtime they bin found another two boys. She bin tell husband to run inside cave and bin make that damper. After crying, old woman bin give them boys that damper and bin tell them to take her to that cave to hunt for that animal.

Two young boys go in that cave and that old man bin finish them with stick. Chuck them outside and drag them off back to camp. That old woman bin say they not my grandson and take them home and cook it and eat them all night.

Old woman bin take him to that cave where that old man hide in corner. Finish, that man bin finish them. Pull them out, take him home and cook and eat them boys all night. They greedy them old people.

Morningtime they bin get up, watching again for more people. Old woman bin start crying and making that damper. After crying he bin give them boys coldsick damper and tell them that same story. *I can't walk. Sometime I go hunting for lungkarr…I'm too weak.* Old woman take them to cave, he in that cave. Them two boys get in that cave and that old man bin kill them, chuck him outside. Take him home and light fire, cook and eat him all night.

Again…another two men bin come. Old woman bin talk about animal inside. They bin tell her:
We not your son, we never seen you before, you can go back home, we from long way.
Old woman bin go back home and the two fellas keep going. They still alive, old woman and old man never bin kill them.

Another two bin come morningtime. That old man bin run fast to cave, old woman start make coldsick damper. Them two fellas bin eat it after woman finish crying.
I'll show you lungkarr…he not far. Sometime I go hunting, it not far, me too weak.
They finish now…dead.

This bin happening for long time, that same story. They bin get good feed from them fellas. They really greedy one, that old man and old woman.

Two fella bin come and they bin thinking:
Where all the people? All gone for good…gotta find them.
They bin have them feelings. Two fella, they clever one, bin come along morningtime.

Get up old man, another two coming, I'll start that damper, that woman bin say. Two fella bin come and they watching that damper. That woman bin cry and after finish she bin give them coldsick damper. They bin break him.
Yuk, that coldsick, that not damper. That not real bushtucker, we not gonna eat it. We not your family, we not your grandson, we don't know you.

They bin talk those two clever men:
We take firestick and light spinifex in that cave, we frighten that lungkarr animal.
Two fella bin get spinifex and put him in that hole. That old woman worry for that old man in corner and bin tell him to get up. She bin tell him that them two boys gonna put fire inside.
What you talking old woman? They bin ask.
Too many flies come in my eyes, woman bin say.

That woman bin talk to husband. Them fellas bin filling spinifex in hole and light him. Old woman bin run away…she bin sad for that old man. He bin cry inside that cave:
Wara, wara, wara, wara…
Fire bin bust that old man eyes and two eggs (testicles). That old woman too old to run far, they bin catch her. Those two boys bin kill old woman, that greedy one.

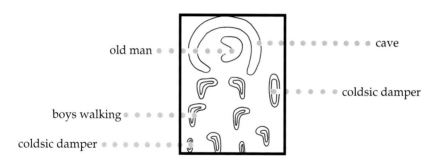

STORIES TOLD AND TRANSLATED BY

Tjama Napanangka

Eagle Man

Eagle man bin have two girls
Cocky and Crow
Crow one bin jealous over that Cocky
Eagle one bin go hunting for animals
Two girls bin go out looking for bushtucker
And the Crow bin say:
That eagle one don't love me he love you more, Cocky
They bin start fight and that Crow bin win.

Crow bin go back to camp
That Eagle bin come back from hunting
He bin ask: *Where my Cocky? Where my wife?*
No…he gone somewhere
That Crow one bin trick him.

Morningtime that Eagle bin go looking for wife
He bin following track
Ohhh…they bin fight
That Cocky one finish…dead
That Crow bin tell me lies
Eagle bin find her dead.

He bin go back to camp
And bin start crying for his wife
That Crow and Eagle bin go lay down
Eagle bin really sad, he bin get big fire
And put it up the Crow's leg.

That Crow bin fly away
Crying from that fire, bin find fire in leg
That Crow bin leave for good
Eagle bin stop there on his own
That Eagle bin stop single…no wife now.

Somebody bin chuck seed in Emu eyes
He bin stop and cry for five days

Eagle bin come from nowhere and he bin listen
Ahhh...somebody crying
Emu bin crying with his head down
Eagle they bin come
Ahh, it Emu that crying. Hey what wrong Emu?

That Eagle bin ask if he can fix him
Emu bin say: *All right*
That Eagle clever man
Eagle bin get them poisonous seeds out
Bin get seed and throw them out.

After Eagle bin ask: *Are you all right?*
Yeah I'm all right.

Eagle bin tell Emu when he see any tree or leaf he gotta run
You can look long way through
When you see any people you gotta run
After that Emu bin turn around and think
Bin thinking about killing people
Emu bin kill all the people with his long arm
It like a knife, got long arm in Dreamtime
That Emu go to another place
He bin kill all the people, even kid
Sometime he kill and eat them.

Eagle bin think: *Where all the people from here?*
Might be that Emu bin kill them, finish them all off
That Eagle bin thinking: *What about we put ceremony for that Emu?*
Everyone bin agree with him.

That Eagle bin come and talk to his cousin-brother
They bin start singing, everyone bin singing and dancing:
Marrangkal tjurr tjurr
Marrangkal tjurr tjurr
You gotta make toilet.

Emu bin dance
Eagle bin get tomahawk and dancing to cut his arms off
He bin grind stone

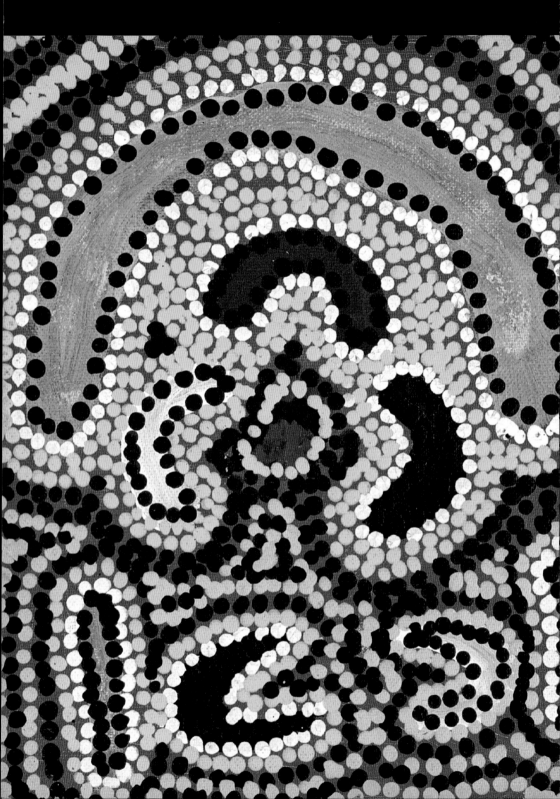

Using spinifex glue to put handle on the axe
Emu bin dancing with arms right out
But that Eagle bin cut them off, they really short now.

That Emu bin make big mob of kid
After that the Emu bin find Turkey
Turkey bin have might be ten kid
Emu bin have more kids
Emu told her kids to keep quiet and she bin go
To look at Turkey.

Emu bin say: *Hey you gotta lot of kid…ten!*
Turkey bin ask: *What about you?*
I got only two
That Emu bin tricking him
Emu bin say: *You gotta have two like me*
Turkey bin kill nine of own kid.

Nothing, Emu bin say, *I bin tricking you. I got ten kids*
That turkey bin start crying and hitting head
Blood everywhere
Turkey bin cry for his kids
Turkey bin cry and take that one kid and go long way
Emu went other way
Never bin seen together.

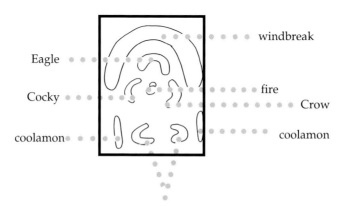

Crow and Cocky hunting

Here, there, everywhere

As little girl we bin start walk from Lake Stretch to Billiluna. From there we bin camp, start walk…mother, father and big mob kids, cousins, aunties. We bin go to Wawula and my daddy bin go hunting. They bin killing two water goanna and me and my cousins sitting home. We bin really hungry. My mother coming and I bin running to catch that goanna. Mother get wood, light it and cook straight away.

It bin raining and us kids bin sitting down in sand watching that water running from Ruby Plains. My cousins and sisters bin see this little dog…
Hello.
My sister grab him that little one. It bin come in the water, still alive.
What we gotta do?
We bin make fire, he bin real cold, shaking, shaking and we bin get him blanket to make him warm.

Mother, aunty and uncle bin go hunting for goanna. We bin sit down and watch him. Two wild pussycat my daddy bin getting. Aunty and uncle bin get three water goanna. We bin happy for that animal, we really hungry. Bin camp there one night and morning-time bin go all way down the creek with that pup. Go to near Ruby Plain creek where we bin find big mob water goanna. Bin cook and eat him and camp there all night.

Morning start again to Ruby Plain, all stockmen there and one manager too. My granny bin worrying for uncle. Kartiya bin taking camel, no mutika. Grandfather bin ask, where that kartiya bin go with five camel, and that somebody gotta go find him. We bin find my uncle and we bin tell him he gotta go down the Canning Stock Route.

We went back to Ruby Plain. Kartiya bin having dinner in house. I bin watching. My sisters bin talk:
You wanna come? What you looking at, camel?
Nothing, I bin say.
I bin watching camel and bin get big stick. They all lying down. I frighten all them camel and they bin run. I bin run down to the creek hiding.

My sisters bin looking and that kartiya bin ask who frighten them camels. I bin watching quietly. My uncle bin rounding all the horses up.
Who bin frighten them camel? That kartiya bin ask him.
My uncle tell him: *No one.*
My sisters bin growling me.
Well that kartiya never gave me watermelon, so I frighten them camel.
They bin tell me I'm naughty and they bin tell my uncle.
Kartiya say:
That girl never ask me for watermelon.

We bin go to Carranya, find big mob watermelon…me on camel. They bin have big market garden, nothing today. Me and my sister run and fill him up water to give that camel. We bin have dinner, then keep going to Old Junction. It wintertime and we bin get plenty feed. We bin camp one night then keep going to another creek to get more watermelon.

Morningtime I bin say I can't ride that camel, I gotta walk. I bin too frighten on that camel. Uncle bin tell me I gotta get on that camel, it too far to walk. We bin ride it to Billiluna. That uncle gotta go down Stock Route to dig wells and kartiya bin take him away to work. We bin stop there at Billiluna Station.

One Aboriginal man bin go hunting, no water…nothing, it hot-time. My uncle bin worrying for that man.
Don't know what time he gotta come back.
He bin go look for that man. Uncle bin walking with water and found his tracks.

That man bin really thirsty, and he bin pass away, died in the heat. My uncle bin crying for him and he bin go back to camp to tell that kartiya that he finish. That man bin have big mob pussycat from hunting…my uncle bin leave it there. Kartiya bin go in camel and my uncle bin show him the way. Dug hole and bury him up. Uncle bin go back to Billiluna after the death.

Pigeon gotta lot of womans

Pigeon bin have big mob womans, maybe twelve
Morningtime in summer
The womans bin tell that old man to get water
We gonna marry you now
He happy so he run to get water and bin bring some back.

After hunting we gotta married with you
They bin say that just to keep him working
Every morning they tell him same thing:
Old man get us water, we go hunting
And after we marry you
Always they bin trick him.

Soon as they bin come back from hunting
With big mob animals
They bin give that old man food
You can cook it for us and after get us water
These two girls gonna marry you
That man bin happy…yes
They bin tell him lies
Old man bin get water
Womans bin drink it and eat that cooked food.

They bin go to sleep
After midnight, everyone asleep
That man bin sneak up to girl and bin touch her
Go away…get out. I'm sleeping
Then he bin go to another girl
Go away…we busy…we tired from hunting
Old man goes back to his camp and lay down again
He get up and try another one
Hey woman, you wanna come with me?
No get out
And that girl bin kick him
That old man keep trying till sunrise.

Morningtime them womans bin tell him to get water
We go hunting and after we marry you
They bin tell him lies
Old man run to get water to give to woman
Then they go hunting
They come back with big mob pussycat and goanna
Old man go get us water, we want to marry with you
He run and get it
Everyone bin drink that water and he gotta cook that food
Everyone eats then womans go to sleep
Good sleep…they tired from hunting.

He look, everyone asleep…sneaks up to another one
You wanna come with me?
No I'm tired
Girl bin kick him out
He goes but try another later
Girl bin kick hard and told him to go away.

Morningtime all the women bin get up
They tell that pigeon to get them water
When we come back from hunting we gonna marry with you
He bin really happy
They bin kill big mob animals
And bin give it to that man to cook
Everyone eats then go to sleep
Womans really tired from hunting.

Old man waits little while
Then gets up and tries another one
He touches her and she kick him out
He waits awhile…try another one
Soon as he bin touch that girl, she kick him hard
He run off.

Old man thinks the womans mad
They bin trick him, tell lies to get water
He bin think that they don't like mans.

Morningtime womans bin tell him to get water
Ahhh…we gonna marry with you
Old man bin get water and gives it to them
Womans bin go hunting
That last time he get water for them womans.

Old man gets big coolamon and fill him up water
He puts that coolamon on head
And the rest of the water he bin cover it up with sand
Old man left all the woman behind
They don't like me…big shame
He bin go bush.

Womans bin come back from hunting, they look
Where that old man? He gone
They bin look around for water, but he never left some
Old man bin take all the water
Where that water?
Womans thirsty for water and they all bin look
They bin see big clouds
That old man bin put rain and all the girls bin running
It raining, but no water on ground
Raining, but it all dry
Not too far it raining, we gotta run there
They all bin run   -
It's bin raining here
Get there but no water
Some walk really weak from no water.

Old man bin tipping coolamon, letting out water and stop
But it all dry
Man bin talk:
You all bin telling me lies
You bin tell me to get water
Now I'm tricking you mob, same like you did to me
After they bin seeing rain they all bin running
Look around and it all dry
Nothing…we sure it rained here
Some girls they bin dead, pass away from not enough water.

Halfway to Balgo from Yaka Yaka, girls bin see big clouds
It gonna rain, we gotta run for that water
They bin get there and it all dry
Something wrong…old man bin drinking all the water.

From there looking again for water
Only two or three womans left now
Ahhh…real rain…look at them clouds
Them girls bin run but when they got there he all dry
Old man bin put it in his head
All dead from no water.

Old Pigeon man bin take his water long way
He bin leave the dead ones behind
Long as them girls bin trick him.

Come to kill, not understand

That white man bin go to Warnku from Sturt Creek. He bin tell all
the stockmen if they wanna go with him and all them Aboriginal
man said yeah. From Warnku they bin start to Kilangkarra and they
bin camp there. Morningtime they bin start to travel to Old Balgo
and camp there.

From Balgo they bin start to Kana Hill…they bin look. Somebody
bin lighting big fire, smoke. They bin go to Tjiitjiwali, then to
Ngantalarra where they bin camp. Morningtime get up and look
fire, they getting closer. One kartiya and Aboriginal stockmen
bin travelling.

From there they bin start to Mantjakulu soakwater. Not far that
fire, they bin get up and look morningtime. From there they bin
start to another soakwater and camp there. Early in the morning
they bin get to that soakwater where old people bin living.

Them people bin come out and look:
Hello, somebody coming with horses.
Men sitting down and boys having ceremony. My grandfather bin
look and he know one of them man. That place them stockmen

bin come out, it called Karingarniny. My grandfather bin talk, that Aboriginal stockman come to get that Napanangka. He Nyangayi's uncle.

That Napanangka bin tell that old man:
He not come for me. Yeah! they after you, my grandfather bin say. My grandfather bin marry that Napanangka but she really sweetheart to that stockman. That girl bin say that she gotta love that stockman. My grandfather bin get wild.

That stockman bin talk:
Hey don't throw boomerang, that kartiya might kill you, he no good. But they never took no notice. My grandfather, he Tjupurrula, bin get real jealous, and bin throw that boomerang at that stockman. That kartiya got wild, it just miss him. Kartiya bin get rifle and bin shoot my grandfather in the chest, poor thing. He bin tell the two wives and daughters they can't cry for that man. They bin sit down quiet and cry real quiet. That kartiya never hear them crying quiet, sitting down. He bin tell all the kids to go get firewood for grandfather.
You fellas can chuck it on top and light him up.
They bin put kerosene on him and light him up. They never cry... all bin sit down quiet.

Some people bin have ceremony. One old man bin go and tell everyone at that place. He bin tell them that Tjupurrula finish, kartiya bin shoot him. They all bin start cry.

That white man with the Aboriginal stockmen and three girl they bin go to Wirparinyu and they bin come out at Mintirr. Big mob bin have big ceremony and the people bin look:
Something might be? Might be devil, that white man.
They all bin run to hill. They bin looking:
Hey what this? Lipi — that mean whiteman.

That white man bin round up all the people, mens and womans, and bin tell them that they good people, not like old man who challenged him.
I bin shoot him.

Kartiya bin tell them that he take them all home. He bin go in front and everyone come behind, go to station.

Near Yaka Yaka

South of Yaka Yaka, Lamanparnta

From Mintirr they bin go to Tjipirr and bin camp there. Fellas bin come behind and that kartiya bin shoot killer for them. They keep going and camp at another Yunpu, near Lanu Lanu, then start again. At Wirararr bin shoot killer and have good feed. From there they bin come out to Pankupiti and all bin have lunch. Went to Kilangkarra Station and they all bin living there...old people and stockmen too.

Other people bin tell us that white man bin shoot one old man in bush over woman. Everyone bin cry. I was little bit walking. My mother and father bin cry too.

That kartiya bin leave some people in Warnku and they bin leave one girl there. They bin take two to Sturt Creek...Nakarra and Napurrula. They still alive, even that Nungurrayi who lives in Nyirpi. The other two living at Billiluna.

Others bin come later after ceremony, to go after that kartiya and Nyangayi's uncle to fight him. They bin have big fight at Kilangkarra 'cos uncle bin bring that white man out to bush. Kartiya went off to Sturt Creek with another mob and left that uncle behind. Everybody bin fight him with spear and they bin cut him.

All the Tjakamarra bin follow that white man all the way to Warnku and bin come out to Sturt Creek. They bin tell him:
What for you bin go bush? Why you bin shoot that old man?
He not a dog!
That kartiya bin say that old man bin challenge him. Tjakamarra bin tell that kartiya that old man was challenging that Aboriginal man. Still they bin fight and they bin hit him. Kartiya bin kill their father, old man Tjupurrula, so he gotta pay. They all leave and that kartiya, he finish, pass away...dead.

Everyone bin go back to Warnku Station, even me. I bin little girl, from bush. Father and mother bin take me and we bin stop there now. I never see my grandpa...I was little baby. Poor my father's uncle...grandpa, they bin cry for that Tjupurrula.

They bin chain them up

From there we bin stop at Mission…Old Balgo
No houses at that place
One brother with some half-caste at Tjumurnturr
Building a well
All us little kids bin playing, making mud
My mother and father bin leave little pieces of bullock for after.

We bin play…I bin see horses
I bin tell mother and father:
Kartiya, kartiya…timana, timana[*]
My mother from sleep bin get up and get big mob dog
She bin run away really fast, bringing all the dogs
They bin run and hide in spinifex, dog and all, keep real quiet.

That kartiya bin round everyone up
Kartiya bin shoot all the other dogs
That Donny, he policeman from Halls Creek.

You fella gotta run, gotta run real fast, Donny bin say
My father bin grab me and we all bin run fast
Kartiya bin get stone and tell us to run
He bin throwing them stones
We bin trick him, he bin miss us with stones
Fast we bin run to Wirrimanu Hill
We bin sit there watching that man
We really tired from all that running
You fella gotta watch out for Nampitjin and them dogs
We bin look out for our mother.

Step-mother bin look after me while they looking for my mother
My father bin find my mother
Which way we gotta go?
I don't know, my mother bin say
From there we bin go back to Taapayi, stopping there.

One kartiya bin come behind
They bin ask: *Who bin killing sheep*
People never said anything…no English

* Horses

Old people from bush…never understand
They bin put them in chain and pull them
Using that wire, all the way to Tjalyiwarn again.

Some people who bin work there bin ask why they got chain
Kartiya bin tell them that they bin stealing sheep
Nothing, these men never kill him sheep
Aboriginal people bin say that, ones working there
Some fella, he half-caste from Beagle Bay
Bin tell that kartiya:
They did nothing wrong.

They bin let him all out
Men bin go back to Taapayi and everyone bin cry
Me and Mati and everyone bin run to Taapayi
Sitting on hill watching for the men.

My mother (Yunitja Nampitjin) and father
Bin take us to Wirrimanu
We don't want to come back to Taapayi
From Wirrimanu we bin go to soakwater
From there we bin went to Lumpu
Then to another place
We gotta sit in bush, not go to house
Paarm Hill we bin stop next
Then Kumputuyikanginu
We bin find white man place
Bin come out same-time with that kartiya police
They bin get off from horses
That Donny one again
He bin put chain on my father and Mati father
They never did nothing wrong.

We bin start crying
They bin take them to house…station
We go to that house
All the stockmen bin come out
They ask the two old men if they bin kill bullock
Nothing wrong, my father bin say:

They bin put chain on me
Stockmen bin tell police them fellas never kill bullock
Nothing…you gotta let them out.

We bin sit down two days camping, waiting
They bin let them out and we keep going
Back to bush.

Left behind to…jump…jump

That boy, his mother bin left him behind
He got double-up legs…you know, walk on them knees
Other people bin find him…they bin look after him
He bin climb tree, catching animal
He bin climb down and cook and eat it.

He man now
From there that man bin go to Ngaranytjartu
Jump…jump…jump
He bin camp there himself
Come out to see bullock
Them bullock bin run, they think he dog
He got no legs, they double up
Jumping like a frog all the way
He bin following the creek

Everyone bin leave him behind when he little
Think that boy gonna die
Anyway he jump back
All the way, creek that man bin following
Bin find goanna for dinner, water one
He bin kill it for supper, take it and cook it
Bin camp there too
Come out to place and bin see men mustering horses
He bin look and find camp
Somebody bin camp here, not long, see that fire still hot
Jump…jump…jump
Scare all them bullock that man
They bin watching that man jumping.

All bin come mustering from station, morningtime
Them stockmen bin look: *Somebody there, must be dog*
Man bin sitting down
One stockman ask him where he from?
I bin come from bush
They bin talking same language
Walmajarri, it same language:
You can go straight up to house…we gotta go mustering
If he bin talk different language they might be shoot him
But he family, got same language
All the stockmen bin tell him to jump to that house.

Some people bin sitting at home
Something coming, might be dog or calf?
Till he bin come close — *No, he Aboriginal*
That man bin ask where his mother live
Somebody bin talk: *He gone to Fitzroy Crossing*
Three days he bin camp at Tjitapuru.

He bin start jump to Fitzroy
From there he bin camp at Number 2 windmill
Then start to Snake 4 windmill
From Snake 4 he bin go to Pamarrtjartu
Asking for mother
He That Way, Fitzroy Crossing.

They all bin talk same language
No mutika for helping him
That double-up man bin camp at creek, big river
Bin cross over it, he dry one
Someone bin see him coming:
We know that man, that Mutayi
Mother one he know — *That my son*
Mother one bin run and grab him
That man bin living there for good
They bin give him rations, no money in them days
He got nice son that old man…he old now.

We bin come to races in Fitzroy
I was having dinner with my aunty…me young girl
I bin sitting down and that man bin jump past
I bin frightened and real scared: *Who that man?*
He your uncle
I don't know that old man, I never see him before
I was drinking tea and I saw this thing
That tea went everywhere
I bin really scared
This time that man bin pass away.

Down the Canning Stock Route

Told by Tjama with Nancy Kungkulu Tax

Soon as it bin dark, wintertime, they bin mustering horses and breaking them in. They bin have two saddle rooms in Billiluna, one for camels and other one for them horses. When people came back from holidays they knew what to do. We had to get grease from the shed and get clean saddles and grease them. We had to wash the saddle cloth and get everything ready. Men do the same for the horses.

Men bin go mustering around Lake Stretch and Kilang Kilang. When that was done they had to brand the cattle. The branding number is UD7 for Billiluna. They still use that brand number. They had to cut their ears and it's called an earmark. The head stockmen tells everyone to pick out the good cattle for sale and then he counts them. The head drover gets his plant ready for droving. We bin go down the Stock Route early fifties. Wally Dowling was head stockman. Another time with Marl Brown, manager for Len Brown.

The cookies get whatever they need, like camp oven, big pots and teapots for kartiya stockmen and Aboriginal workers. They also get big buckets to cook salted meat. The cookies cooked good for the stockmen.

Stockmen bin getting camels ready to start the bullock droving. They bin trap them bullocks for two days and I bin riding camel.

Boys bin watching bullock and they bin come back for lunch. We bin cooking everything, ready for them. Bin getting meat, bread...everything.

Lake Stretch, Nyanatjara, Laman. From there they bin take bullocks to another place called Rilyi Rilyi. From this place we bin take bullock to Lipiri camp and we bin trap big bullock and left cows in camp. They bin take them big bullock for the Canning Stock Route. From this camp we bin start the Stock Route. We bin go in front on camel and start cooking bread. We bin give stockmen dinner like tea, bread, chicken and meat.

We bin camp halfway in route and come out to Lampu Well. Us cookies got water ready for bullock and horses. Put bucket in well and put them on camel then pour them in trough for animals. We bin go in front so cookies get food ready for stockmen. They bin droving about 500 bullock and all bin take it in turns to watch them at night. At sunrise we get up and feed all the stockmen and then keep going. Feed them bullock grass and after, water. Pack everything on camel, swags, water, jerry cans.

From there we bin to Kaningara taking billy mob, water to bullock and they bin come to drink. Cooking all the way and getting up at 4 o'clock to get breakfast ready for them stockmen. It really hard work and I bin put saddle on camel and ride him. We bin have two cookies, two camels, four stockmen and two horsemen. We keep going to all the wells camping halfway. At 9 o'clock it knockoff and some from sleep get up and watch bullock. 10 o'clock someone get up and watch bullock...11 o'clock...same thing. This keep going till 4 o'clock and the cookies get up and light fire to cook and make tea ready, cutting bread. After morning we all keep going.

From Kutjiwarri Well we bin start to another place and we bin getting there first and start billy mob water for bullock and after take him to eat grass. We bin bring back them stockmen for supper and after they bin go back watching bullock. The stockmen watch them all night. It same way, 9 o'clock...10 o'clock...11o'clock... right through the night they bin take it in turns. At 4 o'clock all the cookies get up from sleep and make fire and get tea ready to feed all the stockmen and make everything ready to go to next well.

From Tjimpirinkara bin go to Katatjirkara and halfway we bin make dinner. Same watching go on all night. Morningtime we keep going in front. I bin wearing trousers, hat and stockmen boot. Bin look really funny but no dress to wear cos it rub us in the leg…too much pain.

Bin go to Kulyarri and cook them dinner. Same thing watching bullock. We bin follow them camel track, me in front and Nancy behind. From Kulyarri we bin go to another well and have dinner in halfway road. We sometime camp halfway, it too far to go all the way to the next well.

We bin go to all the wells and same way we get billy mob, water for bullock and camel and start cooking for the ringer. Sameway after supper, man watching bullock, change…change…and 4 o'clock we wake up. It hard work for cookie. One kartiya wake us up. We never got money for working on the Stock Route. They bin give us food and ration. We bin carry all the food on the camel, corn beef too. Sometime that camel work to pull out bucket of water from the well. Sometime we have little engine to help.

We bin go to Natawalu, Kukapanyu, Wataparni, Lipuru Well. We bin billy mob, water, and sometime we bin find Canning Stock Route bush people. I bin getting really sorry for that men and womans. Sometimes we feed them tucker and meat. Stockmen bin shoot killer for them, they bin come with no clothes, nothing, and we feed them everything. Bin give them tobacco too. They all living at Lipuru Well.

Stockmen use to leave food behind for bush people. Them people were always waiting one mile away for kartiya to go. They'd leave behind sugar, meat, damper, salt, tea and flour. This was a new group, it first time they bin run for food. Everyone bin run and take one thing. One person ate all the meat. Someone ate all the flour. Girl bin eat them tea leaves dry. Woman bin eat all the salt and had a headache for two-three days. She was really sick. Some knew how to eat the food so they had to teach the others.

From Lipuru we bin start to another well, not really well it a dry camp. We bin camp halfway at that place and same way watching all night them bullock. On my first trip with Biddy Nangala (she living in Halls Creek now), kartiya bin go in front taking bullock. We bin see him looking at something.

What he looking at? He looking real hard.
We saw this old girl lying down dead and we started to cry.
Maybe she sick one? Biddy bin say.
Someone bin left her behind to finish. From Pankapinyi we bin go to Kily Kily well. Billy mob water and cook for all the stockmen. Morningtime we bin saddle up camel and keep going to dry camp.

We bin find bush people at Kinyu and sometime we bin give them bread. They not wearing trousers, no dress, nothing. We bin give dress to girl there, that Yuka, daughter for Wimitji. We keep going and get to Nyipily. We bin ride camel in trousers and shirt and we never fell off.

All the way down we bin stopping to cook, and feed bullock. Bin camp in Kunawaritji, Nyarurri, Warla Warla. We bin wash clothes in this place and camp two days. We bin let them bullock walk around and eat grass for them two days. Sometime, we cookie work all night, getting bread ready for the morning. From Warla Warla we bin take bullock and camp halfway, watching all night. No water at this place.

In Tjuntu Tjuntu we bin sit, you know, on holiday. Cooking plenty bread, washing clothes for kartiya and walk around a bit. We saddle him up camel and keep going to Wuranu Well and start cooking for the stockmen and everyone. Bin cooking everything, you know.

We bin ride them camel and stop all the way. Bin go to Mamunarra, Raarki, Tiwa, Kalpa and Tjilkipuka. We bin find two girls at Tiwa and we bin give them soap and a good shower. We bin wash their hair and give them clothes. Those two girls, they Nangalas and they relation for Yupinya, from her brother. No one ever got sick on Canning Stock Route. From Tjilkipuka we bin go right up to a creek to Pakitjartu. In this place all the men dig holes and cover them up. Them stockmen bin put meat and tin tobacco in there for after, when they come back.

We bin camp at Well 16, it got kartiya name. We bin camp there getting water and cooking for when the stockmen come with all the bullock. From this well, we bin ride up to rockhole 17 and bin camp there one night watching all the bullock. We bin get up really early and keep going. We bin have dinner halfway and head off to Well 19. A droving bloke from Wiluna bin bring clothes for stockmen and cookie. He bin bring blankets, flour, everything.

From there we bin start to Number 10, coming close now to Wiluna. We bin stop on the way cooking for everyone and watching bullock all night.

Sometime we camp two days, feeding bullock grass and washing clothes. From there we bin take them to Number 5, watching one night and then at a sheep station…it because one of the stockmen lives there in summertime. Bin keep going and at Number 3 we bin shoot killers. Keep going to Number 2, it windmill camp, and then to Number 1. We bin leave everything there and bin riding to Wiluna. He coming close now to big station and we bin camp there one night.

In Wiluna, we bin put them bullock in a train to go to Perth. Cookies bin riding horse after finish bullock run. Sometimes we bin stop in Wiluna for two weeks. Cookie, stockmen and boys go all the way back to Billiluna. After drop off we go hunting with horses getting pussycat and goanna. Kartiya bin shoot plenty bird and we bin make big bird soup…wild cocky, any bird.

I did three trips as a cookie. The second time I bin go down, we bin have big rain, winter bin come. All the stockmen watching bullock. That rain frighten them bullock, all that lightning and thunder. Bullock bin run away. Them stockmen were watching out all night, keeping an eye on them animals. When it got little bit light, the stockmen saw all the bullock were missing. They bin looking at them trees all night, thought they were them animals. Everyone bin sad for bullock, they all finish. We bin thinking:
What we gotta do?

Biddy and me bin put our coat on and get on camel. We bin go looking and rounding up the other camels. Stockmen couldn't find bullock. We bin packing up everything, swag and saddle and keep going to another well. We camp there one night, bin see Yupinya mob. Next day Biddy and me go looking for bullock. We bin go back to Billiluna with 300 bullock that we found with our camels but 500 still missing. It wintertime.

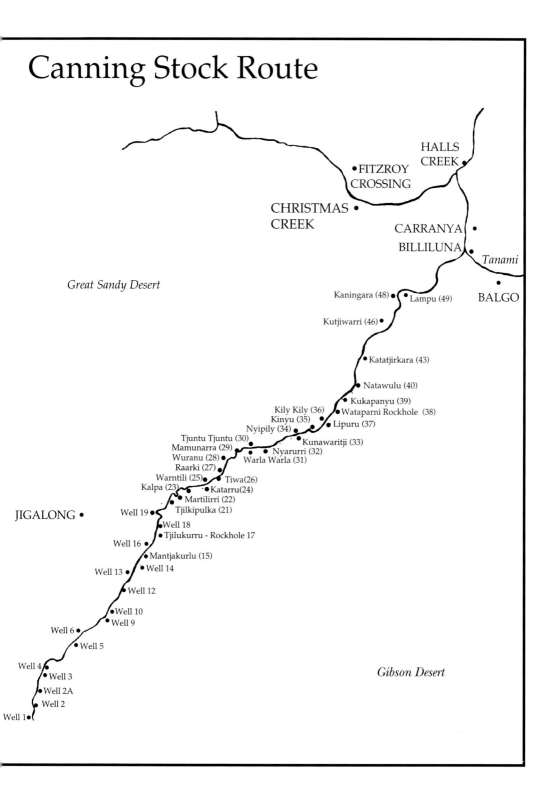

Canning Stock Route

Great Sandy Desert

HALLS CREEK

FITZROY CROSSING

CHRISTMAS CREEK

CARRANYA
BILLILUNA
Tanami

Kaningara (48)
Lampu (49)
BALGO

Kutjiwarri (46)

Katatjirkara (43)

Natawulu (40)

Kukapanyu (39)
Kily Kily (36)
Wataparni Rockhole (38)
Kinyu (35)
Lipuru (37)
Nyipily (34)
Tjuntu Tjuntu (30)
Kunawaritji (33)
Mamunarra (29)
Nyarurri (32)
Wuranu (28)
Warla Warla (31)
Raarki (27)
Warntili (25)
Tiwa(26)
Kalpa (23)
Katarru(24)
Martilirri (22)
Tjilkipulka (21)
JIGALONG
Well 19
Well 18
Tjilukurru - Rockhole 17
Well 16
Mantjakurlu (15)
Well 13
Well 14
Well 12
Well 10
Well 9
Well 6
Well 5
Well 4
Gibson Desert
Well 3
Well 2A
Well 2
Well 1

131

I (Nancy Tax) bin go down the Canning Stock Route with Tjama and one time I bin asleep on that camel and fell over.
That true.
There bin three camel behind me with swag, wood, food and water but they didn't kick me, lucky. My camel was a quiet one but them other ones, they real cheeky mob. Tjama was behind me laughing all the way.

One time they bin leave battery behind, you know for the radio. Them bush people bin looking at it and I (Nancy) seen them cutting it open thinking it was food. They were cutting pieces looking for food inside. No more battery, they bin cut it right up. Bush blackfella didn't understand that battery, never bin see it before.

I remember at Kinyu Well, bush people bin come ask us for killer. That was Yupinya mob and family…all young ones. Kartiya bin killing one bullock and he leave it for them. Them bush people bin spearing wild camel when they bin living on Stock Route.
Hey kartiya, them bush people bin killing one camel, wild one.
It was lost one from long time ago.

Tjama and me we take turns in making damper for the men. Tjama really good cookie. Sometime I make the fire and Tjama light next one, take turns. Me and Tjama bin go down first time as cookie. She bin keep little kangaroo and bring it all the way from Billiluna to Wiluna.
Yeah…
I(Tjama) get bag for that kangaroo and it run and jump into it. Sometime I call it and pull my shirt out and it get in. On the camel I put him in a proper bag and it rides with me. I bin give it to someone in Wiluna.

I bin take sheep on the way home. It lay down like a little baby. Kartiya bin go shooting bird and that sheep bin running. They all bin singing out for that sheep, singing, singing and they bin tell me to go find him. I bin sing out:
C'mon sheep, maaaa…maaaa.
It come running right to me. My little sheep didn't like some people. They bin kill him at Billiluna at Christmas time, poor thing. Everyone bin say it nice meat but I never had some. Naughty kartiya bin cut him, swish, swish on the neck. It raintime, wet season.

The second trip Tjama and me bin go round the Lake Gregory, and my husband had a big punch up with this kartiya and he broke that man's jaw. My husband bin riding the same horse all day and one night. That kartiya bin tell Tax to get a fresh horse. We bin go to Balgo after that fight and that Polly girl bin do second trip. My husband was a good rider and stockman when he was young. After four boys and four girls he getting old. We had eight kids and he's getting old and blind.

One time we (Tjama and Biddy) all bin camping and dingo bin frightening all the bullock. We bin run to kartiya. Them bullock bin running towards us and we have bread in the oven…finish. They bin too scared to think about people. We bin hiding behind tree, other side of camp. Next morning we get up and have a look. All the bread in pieces and footprints everywhere. That kartiya bin sing out: *Why?...why?...why?*

On route we bin find little girl, finish, passed away. Biddy and me bin walk around first and found him lying down. Someone bin leave him here at Wuranu…he real hard. We bin really sad for that girl.

Sometime we bin come back in raintime, at around Christmas time. We get tucker, rations, clothes, flour, tobacco but no money. We have holidays in Billiluna, big ceremony you know…Law time. From there we come back and start work again. The trip would last a whole dry season, seven-eight months and sometime we had Christmas at Wiluna.

STORIES TOLD BY

Yuka Napanangka

TRANSLATED BY

Tjama Napanangka

We bin go everywhere

We bin go hunting bringing lot of pussycat, me little kid then. We bin stay at this rockhole one night and start morningtime…go to another place. Mother and father bin cook food and give it to us. They bin tell us:
Don't finish it too quick.

They bin go hunting for pussycat and we bin get big mob tomatoes, fill him up coolamon. Some clean one open, we bin put stick through and cook on fire. Sometimes dry them out and put in coolamon and cook that dry one little bit and wash in water. Squash him, bit like pancake. After that bushtucker we go hunting around for pussycat and wallaby and bring him home, cook and eat it. Sometime get bushtucker when no goanna and pussycat.

We bin go another place. People went out hunting for big mob animals. We bin living in water. We bin make tjakapirri, bush sandals, for hot-time, summertime. Put him on and walk around. Soon as they bin get dry we put them in water, soak him to make him soft.

From there we bin go to another place when water finish. Make more shoes. We kids bin go out looking for mountain devil and lizard, no goanna around. That mountain devil bin help us by killing them lizards. We bin hunt plenty kid food, kanu, lingka, and wiitji. That mother and father bin bring pussycat and bin give us little animals. Some leave them for tomorrow. Morning, they give the leftovers to kids and they bin tell us not to walk around. It summertime, too hot to walk around, we bin sit down in one place in camp.

From there we bin shift to another place, another soakwater, living water. On the way road we bin kill them pussycat, lizard, wallaby, any animal. Take him and cook it at living water.

It hot-time. Mother and father bin get me water and put in big coolamon. They bin tell us not to walk around:
You can drink this water.

Footprints across our land

They bin go hunting and we bin sit down in shade. Every afternoon they bin go hunting, kill big mob animals, we bin have plenty feed for supper. That leftover we bin leave for next day. It bin too hot for us to go hunting around for little lizard and bushtucker.

Old people sit down, they good hunters, no one ever starving. Mother and father come back with big mob pussycat tied around waist and others in coolamon. Plenty food for everyone. They bin bring back raw and cooked one.

Mother come back with dingo too, we bin have good feed. We bin get this bushtucker, he black seeds, we call him kalpari. We cook them, light them in spinifex, grind him up on stone and make damper. That wangurnu bushtucker, it got round seeds. We bin fill him up coolamon from that woollybutt and put little water and grind it. We bin put this in damper with other seeds, like lukararra, yitakatji, kurrunkampa. We bin make big damper.

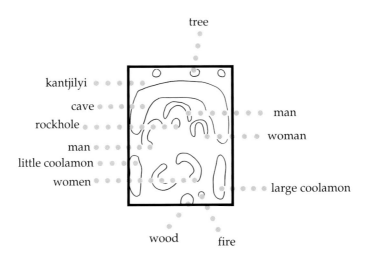

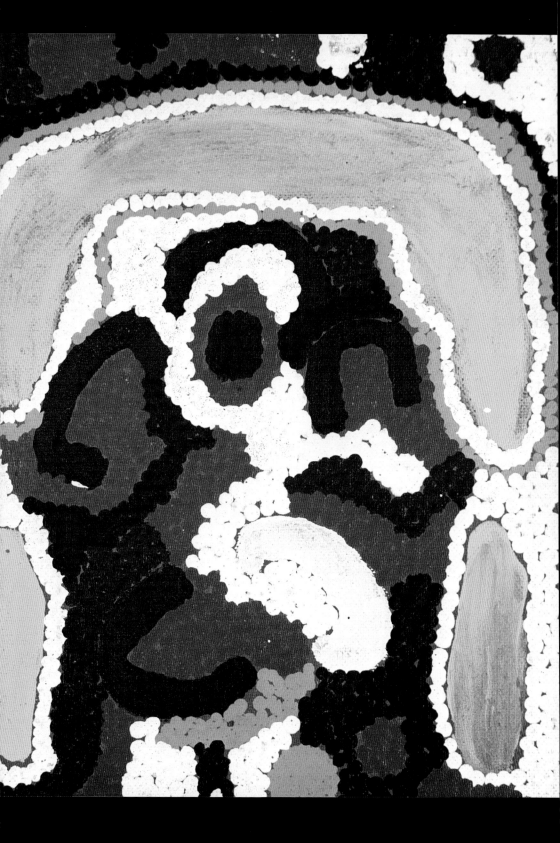

We bin waiting long time

We bin put windbreak
Bin sitting inside under that windbreak
Eating bushtucker
We bin have plenty bushtucker.

Every morning mother and father go out hunting
Sometime they leave us behind
They go out and come back next day
Kids waiting and watching for them to come back
Mother tell us sometime, don't go hunting, it too hot
We bin go to another soakwater
Keep going, all the way.

We went travelling to another place
Bin get lots of seeds for damper
Mother bin go hunting
Looking for goanna
Mother and father bring cooked one, any animal
They bin give to us…it wintertime.

In Tjaalinu one lady in Dreamtime
They bin put in smoke.

In Wawurntjarri
My granny's Dreaming
Man bin get in there
With boomerang broke legs.

In Wirnpupula
Dreamtime man
Woman never bin give him something
Throw bushtucker away
Man bin get spear
Girl bin hold one spear real tight, laughing
Can't throw that spear, too big
Man bin angry, wild
He bin throw boomerang
People bin run in cave, living there now.

Big tree

Summertime bin find another big tree
We call him Tjituwakalpa
Long tree and we bin get them seeds
Put in water in coolamon, squeeze seed and drink it
It like sugar…him big seed.

Mother and father go hunting, look for water
Kids go looking for that sugar
He start raining, wash out that sugar
Finish, can't find him anymore
Good to get before rain.

We go to another place, to Pinangu
We bin living there now
Water bin wash out that tomato and that raisin kanytjilyi
Go to another place
Mother and father bin talk:
Save him something
Don't eat it all that food
We go out for dinner…long way
Come back afternoontime.

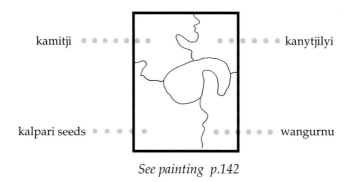

kamitji · · · · · · · · · · · kanytjilyi

kalpari seeds · · · · · · · · · wangurnu

See painting p.142

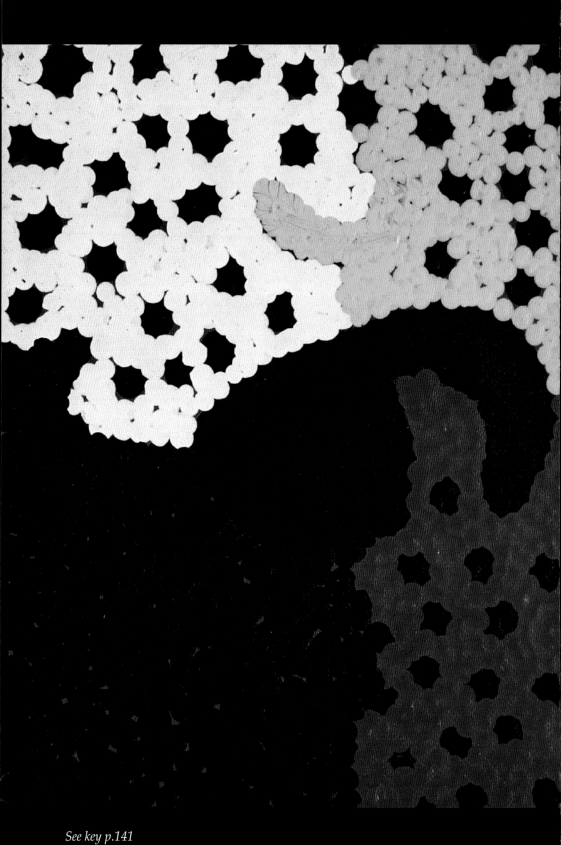

See key p.141

Kid left behind in camp

Mothers and fathers gone out hunting and leave us kids in camp. When we got hungry we go hunting for little lizard, get him and cook it and eat him up. Me little bit big now, I go hunting myself, tracking goanna and kill him. Sometime we bin take dogs. Find them wild pussycat. Soon as mother leave him, little ones go hunting, kill animals, blue tongue, mountain devil, take them home before mother and father come back, cook and eat it.

Mothers, they bring him goannas and blue tongue and father one still long way. Mother come back and feed all them kids. Later on father bring home big mob goanna and pussycat and we all bin happy.

After lunch mother and father go hunting for supper, all the little kids walk and kill little lizard, take him home, cook and eat him. Mother and father come home with goanna and pussycat for supper.

Morning again, father one he go hunting. All little kids go hunting self. All kids bin find bush tomato. Mother go out separate from father and come back with big mob animals. Me big enough to hunt around self. My mother would get soakwater and put in coolamon on her head, take home to camp for hunting in morning. After lunch they go get more kuka to bring home to camp. They all bin happy, all the kids for that goanna.

Morningtime, father one bin go hunting long way way. He bin get and kill an emu, bring and cook him. Everyone happy, they bin say he good hunter. Mother and father sometime bin come back late from hunting. They bin go long way.

Mother and father cook food in bush. They take water and leave it in the bush. Kill pussycat, goanna, fill him up coolamon cooked meat. They come back home later. All the kids get up:
Hello, mother and father coming back.
We all bin run and get that food, it really late…we bin very hungry. They bin bring them cooked one.

Me big now and me take water byself to another soakwater. From there we start to another soakwater, bin go hunting, killing pussycat and sometimes bin find kangaroo — sometime emu too. All the kids bin happy, no coldsick when we were living on bushtucker. We used to cover ourselves up in red ochre and oil from animals… never sick. We camp one night and go hunting around again. Mother and father bin get big mob for supper. We bin have plenty.

Big mob animals

In Wirnpupula
Mother and father bin go hunting
It summertime now — bin get all them kangaroo
He can't run, too hot
They bin bring big mob animals
Some kid they look for mother and father
What time they gonna come
They bin see them and run
My father bin kill kangaroo.

Sometime they bin leave kangaroo in bush
Bring cuts and tail for kids
Then go back and cook it
Too hot to carry whole thing.

Mother and father go back
Kids go hunting, get little lizards, cook and eat it
After that they look for mother and father
We really hungry — get him kangaroo
I'm hungry, give me big one.

He start raining and we make windbreak
Raintime we go hunting getting all them kangaroo
Then we bin shift to another soakwater
This after rain finish
From that place we go to living waterhole
Sit down and camp two days
Then keep going.

In another soakwater we bin get emu
Kill big mob of them animals
Bin living and camping there for three days.

Wintertime we bin get lukararra seeds
We bin finish those black seeds
Plenty bushtucker in wintertime.
Summertime that goanna walk around
We bin have white tomatoes.

Raintime we go to another place
Look for water in rockhole…right, full from rain
We all bin living there
We bin kill big lizard, like blue tongue
But he red one, desert skink
We bin travel to Yinta
That word mean the waterhole on our country.

Yuka Napanangka painting one of her stories

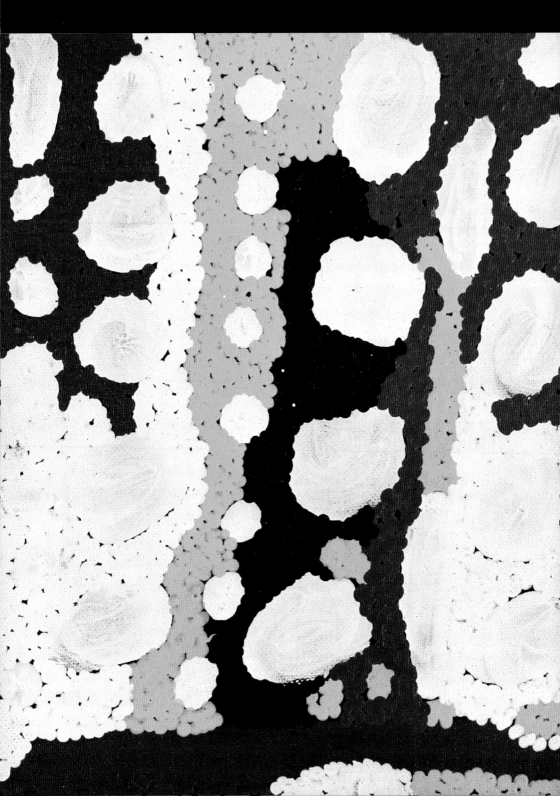

That good honey tree

In Wirnpupula we bin get something like honey
Ngularn…put him in coolamon
It like a flower and you suck that nectar
Sometime we put him inside tree
Someone might eat him
Hide him there for later, supper
We bin go hunting for cat and goanna
Come back cook it and eat it
Sametime we bin eat that ngularn too.

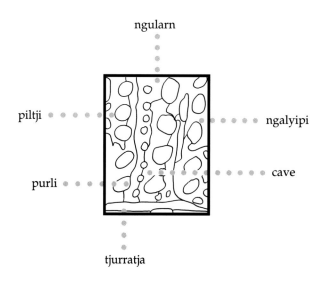

ngularn

piltji · · · · · · · · · · · · ngalyipi

· · · · cave

purli · · · ·

tjurratja

STORIES TOLD BY

Yunitja Nampitjin

TRANSLATED BY

Tjama Napanangka

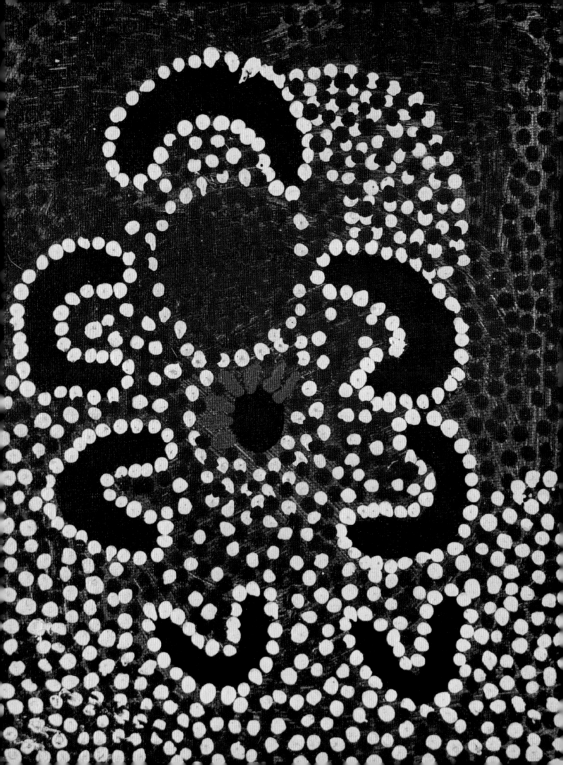

Old man

One old man had two grandson and they bin talk:
We go digging holes for water
Old man bin take them to water
He bin tell them to drink that water together
He bin kill them and pulled them out
Make big fire, cook and eat it
He greedy one.

Old man walk to another place
He bin see fire and he bin find big mob of people
Old man bin tell the people that two boys gotta learn Law
He bin say that he gotta take his two grandson
This brother bin grab them two kids
Put hairbelt and rub him in red ochre.

Old man take them two kids and find soakwater
He start digging hole, clearing sand for water
He bin tell them to drink first together
Old man knocked them dead with a nulla nulla
Made big fire, cook them and eat them
Soon as they bin finish, he want another two boys.

Someone bin lighting fire
Oh my daughter, you got big boy now, he gotta learn Law
I'm here now, we'll grab him today
I gotta rub red ochre and find another boy
I'll take them out, I'm their grandfather
They're lies, he not really
He takes the boys to find waterhole.

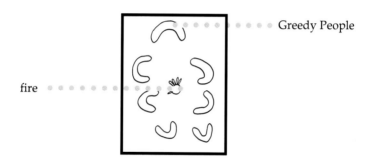

Greedy People

fire

151

Old man digs hole, to clean it
You two can drink together
The boy start drinking together
Old man kill him with a nulla nulla
Pull them out, cook and eat them.

From there, morning he bin look for more fire
He find another mob people
Bin tell them:
Brother, you gotta learn Culture and Law right
We'll grab them, rub ochre and take them to another place
He bin take two boys long way.

He bin tell them to dig hole, clean water and drink together
Then old man kill him, cook and eat him them two boys
He take hairbelt and headband off and throw it away
Sometime he camp for three day and leave parts for supper.

Morningtime, old man look for fire and finds people
He bin say that he here now, their grandfather
And two boys gotta learn Law
Brother-in-law get hairbelt, rub ochre on two boy.

Sister get headband and put him on head of two boy
Old man takes the young boys
Soon as they finish them two boys
They gotta drink water together
Old man kill him with stick
Pull them out of water, cook and eat it.

Mother of that first boy taken, have feeling in breast
I feel no good, something might happen to my son
Mother bin say to follow that old man
He might kill them halfway
Two brothers bin follow that old man
They bin see fires and that he ate boys
They bin find tracks, fire and bones, so they keep going
Them brothers went home, too far
Old man keep killing and he bin finish all young boys
Somebody bin talk from another place.

Old man bin see fire, and he go there
Old men bin see him coming:
What he gonna say? We gotta listen
They look and he got red light in bum
That mean he greedy one
Old man bin say that he here now and he want two boys
All the people bin say: *Leave them, he too greedy*
Everyone bin come…
Clever men and Witchdoctor bin kill that greedy old man
He all red inside, it come all out
He finish that greedy one…dead.

Yunitja Nampitjin and Carl

Blue tongue

Blue tongue bin get up and look
Which way I gotta go, no room?
People out hunting make circle round him
Somebody seen tracks
He bin go this way
That man bin look round
I don't know where he gone, can't find him?

Blue tongue bin walk slowly so people can't see tracks
He bin light fire, that cheeky Blue tongue
All the people bin rush to fire looking for tracks
They find them tracks and followed them and they stopped
They bin lose him again.

Blue tongue bin sing out: *Ayyyyyyy*
Everyone turned round and ran to find him
Look for tracks but they bin lose him
All the way the Blue tongue bin tricking the men
Some people bin say:
We bin see him, don't know where?
They bin look round, can't find him, he gone.

Blue tongue sing out and bin light fire and run
People run to find him:
Which way he gone?
They look round and couldn't find him
There!…Fire…Blue tongue bin light fire
They bin find tracks, then lose them again
After that they bin see him lying down
All bin run to try to kill him.

We saw him there but he gone, we bin lose him again
That Blue tongue bin doing a lot of running around
It bin make his legs and arms shorter
People bin run and look
That Blue tongue, he couldn't run like before
He too tricky, he went underground, no one bin kill him
Big Blue Tongue Hill, other side of Lamanparnta.

Young boy

At Pingirri, long time ago, man bin grab little boy and sent him away. They bin rub that boy with red ochre. Two or three men bin take him to Tjangkapartu. From there he bin come out to other mob in Yarrmanu, take big mob of boys. Then take him all to Piltji. They bin rub all the boys in red ochre.

Mother and maybe sisters bin dancing. Bin take him to Yukurrparli, other side of Lamanparnta, the backway to Mangkayi. Tjirrwilyiwilyi, it's a women's name, place for big Law. Women bin dancing and putting little boys on shoulders and put him down. That little boy, take him to mother and father and after that they put something round his head. That kid Tjapaltjarri bin run away and everyone bin talk. He don't like Law, he frightened for girl and man.

He bin take his headband and hairbelt off. Some people they bin talk: *He run away, we gotta kill and eat him.*

They bin at Yukurrparli place, and they bin go look for him. Finish, they bin kill that boy. The old men, bin going all the way back to Yukurrparli. They bin go underground.

Two men travelling

Two men bin travelling to Yintjirintjiri
Big mob of people living there
They went to Kurrparlintja
These two men, they clever ones
Same two fella that bin make that Willy Willy in Yunpu
They bin sit on the people
Cover them up, finish
Everyone couldn't get up and they all died
Too greedy that mob
From there two fella bin start walk to Kupi and they bin talk:
We'll camp here in Kupi
From there they bin walk to Nyarlungku
Then to Puyupakal.

Kulkarri

Kulkarri bin getting little seed…kuparta
He like a wallaby
He bin cover them seeds up in ground
They safe there and leave him for after
After finish, he built camp in middle
Kulkarri found another mob of seed
He eat plenty and leave some in hole for later
After hunting he makes home under spinifex
He get up morning
And start eating till sun go down.

Every morning go to another place
When he finish seeds, maybe camp three or four days
Dig hole, leave some for after
Morningtime he go to another place
They bin find big mob seeds.

Another animal ask that Kulkarri what he bin eating:
Oh you can eat it, too hard for me…teeth no good, can't bite him
Kulkarri next morning go to another tree
He bin finish them seeds
Then another tree, all like that.

Kulkarri's daughter ask her mother what he had
Mother one bin give some of that bushtucker to daughter
Daughter bite it:
Too hard mummy, you bust him
Mother bin crack seed and daughter eats them
Daughter one too little to bust them
Little girl sit down at home waiting
Mother go hunting and bring some back for kid
That seed like a peanut
It too hard for biting
Little girl grown up and she bust them herself
Every night-time they bin eat them.

STORIES TOLD BY

Yutjuyu Taampa Nampitjin

TRANSLATED BY

Tjama Napanangka

Rukapirla tjurrurlilpi ngarlku panirra

After supper we gotta finish you mob and eat you

Long time ago, someone far away bin light fire. Somebody can go and look for them. A man go and picking up the people and telling them to come and have corroboree in Yunpu place, other side of Lamanparnta.

They bin bring them to Yunpu, they sit together. Yunpu man bin say: *We gotta start dancing and learning.*

That women bin grab a big baby, who came for ceremony, he bin look at that baby and kiss him and he dead. Yunpu — greedy one. They get another baby and give it to the mother whose baby just died. They bin give her Yunpu kid. That mother looked at face, that not my kid. More kids bin get grab and kiss. Dead.

Yunpu people kill everyone, all finish, and they eat them. After that, soon as they bin kill all the people, they bin talk: *He not my family, I'm not granny, aunty, mother for him.*
All the greedy one say that about the people they just killed. When the old mans bin dance, they get pole and break his legs. Yunpu people bin doing that to all the good people.

The Yunpu people looking for more fire, see if anyone light fire. *Run and go get him, have ceremony here.*
Bullshit, all greedy ones, they tell lies…true. They run and get people with big mob of kids to dance, have ceremony. Yunpu people tell them to sit down together: *I'm your granny*
Liars, not really related. They dance.

Morning, at sunrise, they killed whole lot, kids and all. After, they cook and eat all the people. Then they start dancing. Watching for fire…watching…watching…they see one.
Go get them and bring back to Yunpu, we can sit down together close and dance.
Everyone bin dance all night, and at sunrise Yunpu mob bin kill them all and eat them…finish, kids and all.
Two men bin come. Clever men. Singing and talking.

Gotta go look for people. Yunpu bin kill them all.
They bin come to Yunpu, watch and listen to singing.

Rukapirla tjurrulilpi ngarlku panirra
Rukapirla tjurrulilpi ngarlku panirra

Them two old fella bin talk.
That's a greedy song. Not good song.

That Yunpu mob bin say:
We gotta get them two fellas, big mans. They gotta sit with us.
Two men bin sit quiet and they bin listening to mob singing that
greedy song. They bin talk:
Not good people, nothing here, no people, greedy ones bin finish
all of them.
The two men bin move from them greedy ones. They bin sing for
Willy Willy. Greedy one can't see, too much dust. They bin make a
big hole, they all bin go in, mans, kid, all people. All finish, shut
him up the hole. Yunpu people all bin go underground to
Canning Stock Route.

Two fellas bin looking round Yunpu camp. They bin see blood,
bone, liver, little baby head and they bin get sad for the people,
they were good people. Two fellas, they bin keep going, they bin
travelling to La Grange.

See painting p.162

Boomerang

Another two men come and look round
Why no one walk around
Everyone hiding, big mob of people
Two men threw boomerang everywhere and everyone get up:
Hello, someone bin throw boomerang
Big mob say.

They bin make holes in caves
That mob didn't give them two fella karnti…bush potatoes.

Big dreaming fight

Lirrwati, is where they bin stop and living, in the Dreamtime
Tjapanangka bin watching woman laying down
Woman bin born little baby.
He bin say:
You want to come with me, I'll take you
Woman bin getting baby
And all bin running away with the new baby
That Nungurrayi bin ask Tjapanangka:
What we gotta do?
They both bin kill the baby and kept going.

Tjangala, he bin waiting for his woman and baby
He had long hair and look sad way:
Man and woman bin here
He bin find that Tjapanangka and they start fighting
They bin cutting each other in a Tjakurri — waterhole place
Cutting each other on legs with rocks.

Tjangala bin kill that Tjapanangka in Pintjuyangku
He finish…dead he bin cover him up in sand.

Tjangala bin go back and get that women:
Come on we gotta keep going
The two bin drinking water and keep going.

Everyone at camp bin get up, they bin see lot of hawks
Where's that other man, they bin kill him
Everyone bin rush for that man and woman and kill them
All the way
Finish that two
That mob bin kill man and woman
Because they bin kill one man
Big mob people went to Kamirarra and from there
To Nuntalpi
Then they come back to Lirrwati
They all living there now
All bin go underground
Small round hill at that place, this side of Piparr.

Yunitja and Yutjuyu Nampitjin telling stories at Yaka Yaka

Emu dreaming

Emu bin making nest for eggs
After that he bin go hunting, he drinking water
Come back and make more nest
Big mob of Emu, make five nests in circle ready for laying egg
Mother bin listen first
Oh he big now
Then pik...pik...pik
Mother bin bust him and put him down to get dry
Then another one, then another one, ten or eleven egg.

Mother bin teach hims how to walk that funny way
That emu move and then shake them feathers
Moving shoulders back and front
The baby ones, watching mother shaking
And walking funny way
Then they follow mother on a little walk
After they take him all hunting
Eat little munturu seed, that red round one from the tree
All little baby, they eating
Go back home for water.

Every summertime mother bin bust eggs
Mother take little ones hunting
She teach them to shake and talk
Purrrr...
They bin do same way
Sometime they run to the tree for tucker
Run and eating and finish them
Go to another tree, find him berries, eat and run.

They little bit big now
From hunting, come back for water
And go back again in morning
Eating and learning to run
They run and get little bit strong
After come back, drink water and lay down
Morningtime, they learn to run little bit faster and
Get little bit strong.

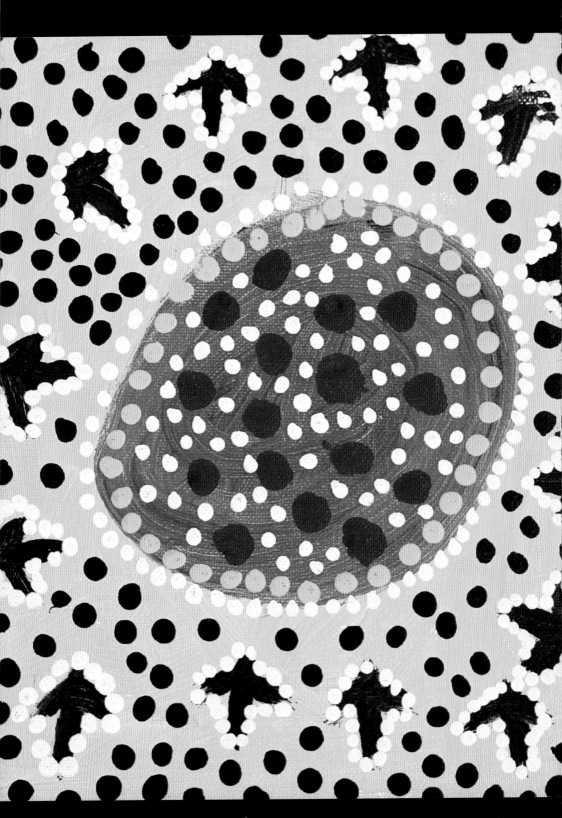

From Mina near Mangkayi they bin go to another place
From hunting, everyone full eating bushtucker
Little baby ones tired and lay down and wait for mother
Morningtime, mother wake him all up
Go to another place
Always they keep going.

Yaparru, living there now, it Dreaming place
They hunting around
They bin go underground through a hole and keep travelling
Come out somewhere, long way way
They bin come out in Kinytja, east way
They bin go for good to Mangkuru, from that Kinytja place.

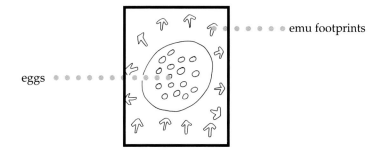

STORIES TOLD BY

Kuninyi Nampitjin

TRANSLATED BY

Tjama Napanangka

Big fight

Lirrwati, Kuntanyintja
Two fella bin start fighting, cutting
Tjapanangka and Tjangala.

All the way they bin fighting and cutting
All bin cutting...long fight they bin having
Bush knife, tjimarri, white stone...using that to fight
That place got three name
Lirrwarti, Mangkayarra, Kuntanyintja.

Ngarntanyirna is a creek
They bin have long fight over woman.

That little bird, he like eagle...not really eagle
Puluwarra bin watching them two men
Fighting
Sametime it bin raining
Big raining.

That Tjapanangka and Nangala bin kill baby:
What we gotta do, he got no father?
We gotta kill him.

That Tjangala bin kill Tjapanangka
That Tjangala bin win
Kurkal Kurkal Hills...where that bird living
He living there now
Bin go underground.

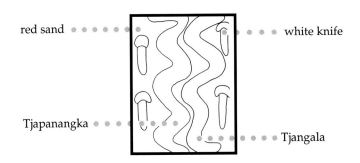

red sand ● ● ● ● ● ● ● ● ● ● ● white knife

Tjapanangka ● ● ● ● ● ● ● ● ● ● Tjangala

STORIES TOLD BY

Yupinya Nampitjin

TRANSLATED BY

Yirtawu Napanangka
Marri Nakamarra Matjital
Tjama Napanangka

Hunting out

We go hunting for tjaakampa, bushtucker. We broke tree and them seeds fall over in ground. Get him black seeds and fill him up from every tree. Put in coolamon and sort him out. Go to another tree and get more black seeds…break him trees, same way, fill him up coolamon. We bin take him home, some eating and leave some for after. Then we bin go back to get some more…fill him up for after. Put in punyanyi, little leaves to keep them safe for after. We didn't have bag then.

Go to another place now, it living water and we bin stay there, till that bushtucker finish, kamitji, pura. We bin start walking to another place and bin find bush tomato in that place. I was little girl and my mother goes hunting, fill him up coolamon and bring him home. All the little kids waiting at home. Some man bin go hunting for pussycat and goanna. They bring big mob and they cook and share it out.

We start to another place, get them bush tomatoes again. Sometimes if there no tucker we go to different place and get another tucker. Some fellas go hunting out. At other place we bin get plenty bush onions, fill him up coolamon, take home and cook it.

Our mob bin walk to living water on Stock Route, near Warla Warla, getting tomatoes, pussycats and goannas all the way. All the womans get bushtucker and the mans get all the animals. We keep going and bin come out to Warla Warla…it Well 31 on Stock Route. We bin come out from bush to that place. At this place we bin get plenty bush onions, digging and filling up coolamon.

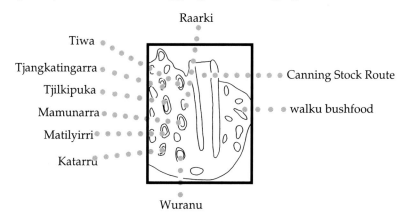

From there we bin start to Tjuntu Tjuntu…all bin walking. All bin find that red walku. We bin start walk that Canning Stock Route to Wuranu, digging hole looking for seeds. Bin get some and chuck him on ground, wash him in coolamon and put on flat antbed to dry him out. That mungily we bin get. We bin have plenty feed. Mans get dinner, go out getting wallaby and wife grind them seeds and bin make damper for husband. He have it when he come back…it really late.

Morningtime we bin walk to Wuranu well. We drinking water, then go past to another place, Raarki. From there to Tiwa well. Some people bin living there and we all bin stop there together. Same-time go hunting getting bandicoot. We bin get plenty food, that's why we bin stay there long time.

We bin travelling, travelling, travelling. To Katarru, we bin stop for while and from there to Warntili. We bin get plenty mungily, wash him out and put on claypan to dry. Soon as they dry we get him, it like hanging out clothes. Then we grind him on stone and make a big mob of damper. We eat the lot and then go out looking for more. Bring him home, wash him, put on antbed. After it dry we go get him. We find pura, it bush tomato…too much bushtucker we bin getting.

We bin go back to Katarru. Getting bush onions from wintertime to summertime…till rain bin come out. We bin stop in that place. At Kalpa Well we bin find no tucker, we starving. Keep going to Martilirri, it Well 22. After we bin go to Pintulurru, I'm a big girl now, married you know. Too much pussycat, too much goanna. I'm good hunter.

Every morning we go hunting for the same tucker. Bin get rabbit there too. From there it long walk to Tjilkipuka and then we bin go to another well. Stockmen and all bin taking bullock to Wiluna. They bin shoot killer for our mob. That next place we walk, white man call it Water 17. It really called Tjilukurru Hill, it got rockhole. We bin drink water then keep going.

From there we bin go to Well 18 and on the way, road, bin get pussycat for dinner. Keep going and camp halfway in dry camp, it got no water. Bin get to Well 19, Mantja, and then walk to

Tjangkarti. We bin camping there and them stockman bin tell us to go behind them.

Only cookies can go in front, too much humbug with the bullock. Bush people can't go in front, they might get into trouble. When anybody go down that Canning Stock Route, they can't go all the way to Wiluna. That government funny mob. Only cookies can go all the way to Wiluna. Bush people might get into trouble.

Marnkalpa

They were picking up the seed part of spinifex…marnkalpa
Cleaning it and putting it in the middle of the fire
Hit the spinifex with branch, skinny stick
And the seeds fall underneath
Take the long stems and throw them out
I was doing a good job, it was like food
We killed that spinifex with a stick, good food
When I get some for Michelle, Mark Muura
They'll give me a mutika for that…might be.

We gathered them, and clean him up
Put them together and hammer them up with rocks
Get a stone from the fire and put it in the pile of seeds
Then cover him up
Smoke comes out, then grind him up
That's what we do
Spinifex still growing in the desert.

I was a young girl in the bush
That food from the desert, don't get it very often
Big food, it feed the whole family, now I eat white man food.

Two men got some spinifex, we call this one tjinalpa
They cooked it and when they tasted it, it wasn't good
It tasted like bitter one, salt maybe
When it's heated up it's like glue, and when it's cold
It's like cement.

They use to tie things together with that spinifex glue
Use kangaroo string with it too
They used to make those axes
Joining the pieces together, wood and stone
So they started using it to fix things
Spears, spear-throwers, boomerangs
Even cracks in coolamons…true!

The two men kept going to another waterhole
Took that black glue they made with them
They moulded it into a round ball shape
It easy to carry
That spinifex was growing at Canning Stock Route as well… all over
These two men travelled and dropped seeds everywhere
Might be they fell by accident.

Nakarra Nakarra

Waiting

I was a little girl
Mother go hunting self
Kill golden bandicoot and cook him up
I gotta stay home
Mother and father bin come back from hunting
I bin sitting in camp waiting
They bin come back with plenty kuka
I bin get real happy
Cook it and they bin give me some
I bin eat that goanna
I full up…go play around by self
Mother bin leave me more meat for after
I follow mother for hunting
Mother bin say she go far away
I gotta go back and sit down on self
We all happy when mother come back
She bin have two daughters
My sister little bit big, I'm really little
We bin see mother coming…we bin run
Sister bin get wood for mother
Light that fire and cook goanna
Pull him out and eat him.

Someone bin kill that sister in bush
Only me now
My mother bin look after me
Mother bin take me hunting…bin learning all the way
After lunch mother bin leave me behind
Killing all the goanna for supper
Bin come back late.

They bin kill my sister…snake or something
Mother bin leave us self when she bin go hunting
No mob of people camping with us
No flour, only bushtucker
Never bin sick…no coldsick in the bush.

I bin leave my mother behind
I bin grow…big enough now

I bin go to Nyarurri
On Canning Stock Route
They bin pass away…people bin kill them
I come back for mother
Everyone bin tell me that she pass away
I bin start cry for mother
Cry…cry…cry…
All night for my mother
I bin travelling all around, no mother
Nyinmi, Tjintarr…him dry country
Yutjantjarra rockhole
Travelling, travelling, travelling.

Killer feeds all

We started by killing a killer and going off further down towards the Canning Stock Route. Came last to the camp then decided to have dinner. Had dinner and then got up with camels. We saw another lot of people shooting a killer and the mens hanging up that killer in the boughsheds to dry.

We were droving bullocks and we gave them some water. We took those cows east, that side, then in the eveningtime brought them back to camp. We put the cows back in the yard to have a rest. They asked our mob if we had killer for travelling and few of the mens said: *We already had one. We got some of the killer and cooked them up and kept some so we can eat it when we were travelling.*

Started going south and kept going with camels and bullocks, kept on going that side. Kept going, following those people and some were behind us…there were three groups. We kept following them until they came to a camp. We had a few in-laws in that camp and they gave us tucker, then we went to sleep. Few of the mens got up in the morning, got some of that killer and put it on the camel. Took some of the camels which didn't have people and got them to sit like camels sit, they have good rest. Made kitchen to make dinner. Few got on the camels to go get wood for the camp and then had dinner. Took some of the camels out for a walk and when it got late put them back. We gave the people supper and then went to sleep.

Got up morningtime and went to another place. Saw another lot of people in that place and we gave them the killer that was on the back of the camel. We didn't want to stop...kept going. Kept going to Raarki and gave another lot of people meat from that camels back and kept going. Got on the camels and put wood on them too. Got halfway and made fire and had dinner. Gave the camels water, took them for a walk and then brought them back.

We up early and some of the camels started to wander off. We followed them and some of the mens got on other camels and went to get them.Went further south and saw mens talking. They were sitting around the fire. We saw them at Warntili and they gave us damper and some food. We gave them little bit of killer. We slept there one night. Early morning, went to another place and arrived there morning.

Arrived at Katarru and the mens give the camels water and the womens sit under a tree in the shade. Then to Kalpa and then I went to my sacred place, Martilirri, and we left the camels to drink. Sitting around the fire when they gave us meat and a leg of the killer, cooked it and saved some for later, to eat on the way. Stopped at another place, Tjirkungka and camped there, ate some of the left over meat and kept going. Saw some of the people on the way and gave them cooked meat. We camped there with those

people. Few of the mens took killer in front and went out hunting and got bush meat, pussycat, cooked and ate it for dinner then we kept going. We made some of them bough-sheds, gave the camels and bullocks water and kept going. We stopped at Tjirli Windmill.

Came up to another place, too much spinifex, and we were camping there. We saw two kartiya and they gave us some killer. They saw we were travelling with no meat, so they shot a killer and gave us some. They gave us some damper and left over cuts and tail of the bullock and kept going. Came to a place called Warntili and camped near there. Few of the mens still coming with the bullocks and camels and slept near the lake. There were also small camels and we left those little ones to have a rest and give them water. We left some of the people near Well 11 and told them to stay there.

We saw Len Brown, Mallee Brown's father, coming behind and he passed us on a horse. He growled on us because we shouldn't be there. He told us we might scare the cattle — it is cattle country. We went to Well 9 and saw policemen and had an argument with him. The police told us to keep going, we were camping in the wrong place. Well 10 now…back and forth, we were travellers. We camped there and digging for soakwater and we decided to stay there for a while.

I tell them

They told me, my two sisters was digging up for yams to go north. I told them I wasn't going to Wiluna. I wasn't going to Kanirrki, it too far. I was in Warnku. I was telling them where the places were…that side…other side. I was doing a lot of hunting around.

We went to Warnku and stopped there for awhile. I came up to my country, the two hills, then to another place, Tjankarti…lot of spinifex there. That man Len Brown was following us. He came up behind and saw only womens and asked why the mens dumped all the womens. Those men gone hunting. Womens told him they were left there while men went hunting.

Yupinya collecting wood

My Country

This is a country one…walking around
Yurunguny rockhole, Tjaliwaya, Tjaalinu rockhole
My country
Deep rockhole there
Drink that water, then go hunting around
Come back and drink more water
I was a young girl
Then we went to Tjunparntja
Got frogs, sand ones
When we ran out of water, out hunting
Go back to hole and get more
Then go out hunting again
Then we travelled back to Kuntupangu
When we finish water, go to billabong
Put leaves on the billycan to cool it down
Sun go down
Back to billabong.

Out hunting always dry
We had kids too
After sun go down
Went back to Tjunparntja
Then to Kurtuwarangu
Then to Kunyulurru
Camped there and later went east
Then to Tjanpirku
Dreaming story there
Women saw two snakes fighting, two Tjungurrayi
Them snakes coming from Tjukula way, going to Kulykurta
From the sand dunes — real ones
Took no notice of those snakes
Drank water from the rockhole
Then we moved to Minyurr
Stopped there and did some hunting.

Then to Mantilatjarra
Nyaakarlpa, Nyila…big rockhole
Between Well 33 and Jupiter Well
Just went to Nyila rockhole, kids and all
Getting plenty lukararra, white seeds too
Then to Ngawuli rockhole…real big
Stayed awhile
Tipiltju, moved there
Yalanytjirri, then to Tjintarr rockhole
Grandmother bin find me there
Lot of walking
Plenty water in my country…
That's My Country.

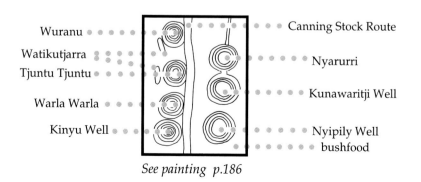

Wuranu	Canning Stock Route
Watikutjarra	
Tjuntu Tjuntu	Nyarurri
Warla Warla	Kunawaritji Well
Kinyu Well	Nyipily Well
	bushfood

See painting p.186

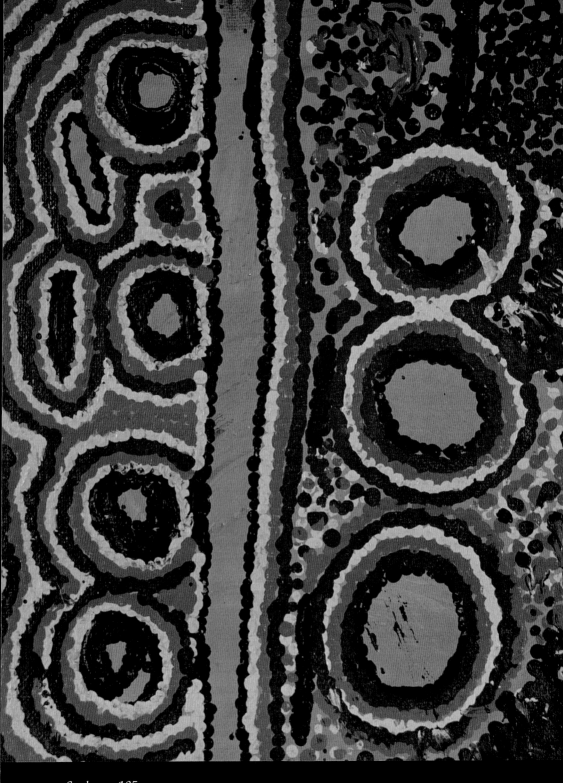

See key p.185

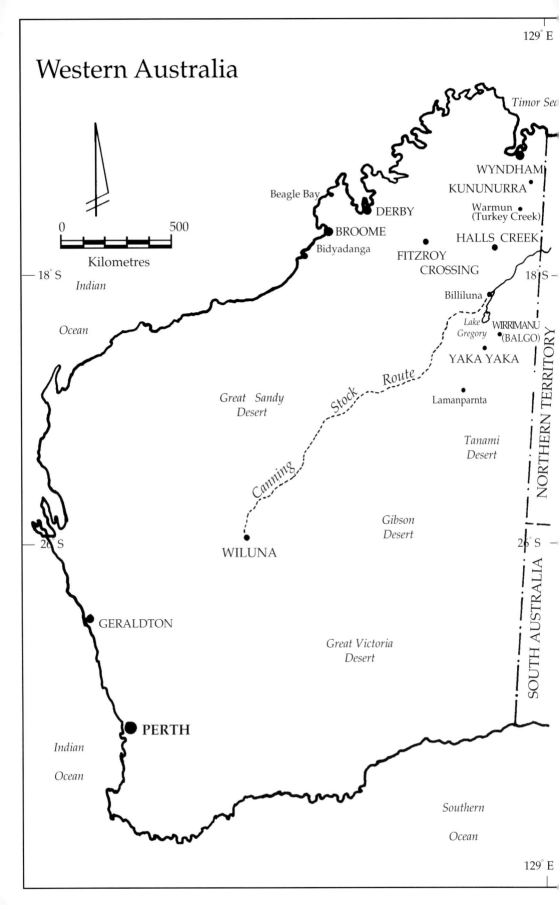

Language Groups
Central - Western Australia

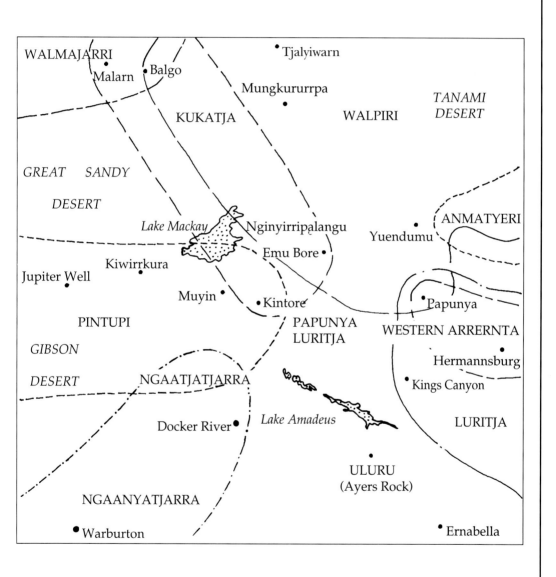

Detail from a map of current distribution of Central Australian languages, reproduced by permission of the Institute for Aboriginal Development, Alice Springs. This map is based on incomplete information and should be used with care.

Glossary

Coldsick	Cold/flu 8, 52, 101, 103, 105, 143, 179
Coolamon	Bowl/container made from wood 1, 6, 7, 8, 9, 10, 15, and throughout
Kakarratuly	Red Mole 73, 75
Kalany	Short black wallaby 14
Kaliny Kaliny	Honey Grevillea 84
Kalpari	Rat tails. Leaves chewed with water in mouth and resultant mush spat out on to burns and sores. Leaves also chopped up, ground on stone with other leaves. This mush is rubbed on chest as remedy against respiratory complaints or on parts of body in pain 138, 141
Kamitji	Berries, berry juice, fruit juice 83, 141, 175
Kanytjilyi	Bush raisin. *See* Kintinyka, Kumputjirr, Wangki 8, 9, 138, 141
Kanu	Lizard; skink 136
Karnti	Bush potato 163
Karrulykura	Mulga apple 21, 24
Kartapila	Feeling in the foot 87
Kartiya	White person *see* General Index
Killer	Cattle for immediate local consumption, cow or bullock 50, 120, 176, 180-82
Kintinyka	Bush raisin. *See* Kanytjilyi, Kumputjirr, Wangki
Kuka	Meat 9, 34, 40, 43, 49, 50, 57, 78, 79, 80, 82, 83, 86, 143, 179
Kulila	Listen, look around 76
Kulkarri	Little wallaby 157
Kumputjirr	Bush raisin. *See* Kanytjijyi, Kintinyka Wangki 25
Kunatilti	Goanna *see* General index
Kungkala	Rub, grind, light fire. Fire stick 60, 79, 80
Kuparta	Plum bush 157
Kurturtu	Heart 89
Kurrkarpi	Desert oak; seeds eaten, usually when green; cones lightly roasted to release seed. At certain times, usually in warm weather, nearly mature cones release sweet white substance – either eaten immediately or cones soaked in water and liquid drunk. Water can be obtained from roots. Wood used to make clubs, special heavy fighting spears. Inner bark used to make ash for chewing with bush-tobacco. Cold ash from burnt leaves rubbed on sores anywhere on body. Moist inner surface of bark also rubbed on sores. Sweet substance exuded from cone-like fruit, is used medicinally, to alleviate headaches and light-headedness due to lack of water, both caused by walking great distances
Kurrunkampa	Naked woollybutt. *See* Wangurnu 72, 84, 138
Latju	Witchetty grubs 80
Lingka	Snake 136
Lukararra	Type of sedge grass. A sweet food when ground, mixed with water and made into damper and cooked in ashes. Ground seed also mixed with any kind of fat and applied to sores anywhere on body 1, 40, 57, 138, 145, 185
Lungkarr	Wallaby 101, 103, 105

Manakarratja	Bush tobacco 53
Mangarri	Vegetable food, food in general 69
Mangarta	Quandong, native peach, plum bush. Stone or nut contains an oily kernel. Ground to paste used medicinally to rub into body, particularly back and head for aches and pains 21, 22
Marnkalpa	Spinifex, spinifex resin 177
Mingari	Mountain devil. *See* Minirri, Tarlkayarri 48
Mingatjurru	Golden bandicoot 179
Mirnirri	Mountain devil. *See* Mingari, Tarlkayarri 48
Mungily	Type of Acacia. Seeds from this plant eaten raw, also ground on stone and inserted up nostrils to alleviate pain in nose. Leaves rubbed on any part of body for external sores or internal pains. Leaves also macerated, mixed with water and applied liberally to sores. Plant material in dwelling construction provides dense shade 15, 176
Muntalya	Like onions
Munyurn	Plumwood, sandalwood tree. Shells removed from roasted seeds and ground kernels made into edible paste. Paste also rubbed into hair, beard or whiskers to make them beautiful and promote growth. Stem, roots used as fire-saw and drill. Red juice squeezed from fruit sometimes used as dye. Seeds ground up, mixed with fat or water, rubbed on sores 21, 68, 69
Munturu	Shrub without common name. Seeds used for damper 165
Nunpi	Little wallaby 82
Ngalyipi	*Crotalaria,* also Green birdflower, Sturt's desert pea (*Clianthus formosus*), Parrot plant, Rattlepod Birdflower. Uses: bush-sandals; rope (woven) to carry heavy loads and as lashing in spear construction; fire-saw, fire drill; (medicinal) bark rubbed on sores and to reduce swellings; decoction of leaves as eyewash; plant used for binding or wrapping sores; painful areas; leaves bruised to obtain a few drops of liquid; placed in an aching ear 147
Ngarawara	Native fuchsia. *See* Ngularn 24
Ngularn	Poverty bush, native fuchsia. Sugar bushtucker. Flower pulled off and base sucked to obtain small amount of nectar; flowers gathered, rubbed between flat stone and hands and eaten; (medicinal) leaves and branches ground up, mixed with water, rolled into a ball, eaten as remedy for general sickness or rubbed on painful areas 4, 8, 84, 147
Nyirtu	No common name, erect shrub. Seeds from this plant roasted, eaten. Also pierced and used as necklace beads 57
Nyupa	Spouse, partner 73
Nyuwari	Plum bush, plum bush seeds 24
Pampilanytji	Beans 76
Paranti	Desert wallaby *see* General index
Pintitiri	Bandicoot 82
Pirnkiwarnu	Tobacco plant found in caves 53
Pukara	Desert Thryptomene. Dew collected from flowers in cooler months 80, 84
Puluntari	Fungus species, type of truffle. Fluid squeezed into sore eyes and on sores. Elderly rub fungus into armpits like deodorant stick. When rubbed in hair, prevents growth 25
Punyanyi	Leaves 175
Purarra	Honey ant 24, 25

Pura	Bush tomatoes 176
Puti puti	Shrub with brightly coloured calyx, bud covering.
Soakwater	A place to dig for water *see* General index
Sorry meeting	Mourning and wailing for deceased person 31
Tali	Sandhill
Tarlkayarri	Mountain devil. *See* Mirnirri, Mingari 48
Timana	Horse 121
Tjaakarmpa	Bush currant 25, 175
Tjakapirri	Bush sandals 136
Tjangala	Dreamtime beings, also skin group *see* Name and General index
Tjapanangka	Dreamtime beings, also skin group *see* Name and General index
Tjalapa	Great desert skink 68
Tjarralaparlparl	Pigeon 61
Tjatupitji	Prickly shrub, bush tomato 83
Tjinalpa	Soft spinifex, spinifex gum or glue 177
Tjipari	Sturt Creek Mallee. Medicine tree. Uses: natural antiseptic, fire-saw, medicinal smoke source, seeds eaten without preparation for general sickness leaves crushed, boiled, put on sores, cuts, burns 52
Tjira	Oil/fat, any cooking oil, hair oil 78
Tjirrilpatja	Bush carrots. Swollen roots, eaten raw or cooked in hot sand and ashes. Also eaten by emus 15, 57
Tjituwakalpa	Corkwood species 141
Tjurnta	Bush onion 14
Tjurratja	Tobacco 147
Walku	Quandong, Native Peach, Plum bush 21, 24, 175
Wangki	Bush raisin, native tomato, wild gooseberry *See* Kanytjilyi, Kintinyka, Kumputjirr 21, 25
Wangurnu	Naked woollybutt. Seeds ground for making damper 138, 141
Wanapiti	A type of sedge. *See* lukararra
Wara	Expression of surprise
Warakatji	Snake vine. Leaves or latex from stem is rubbed on spear wounds and skin lesions. Leaves also chewed for bad colds. Tinospora stem wound around stomach to alleviate pains...when used like this, leaves broken off and latex exudes from break. Considered to make a person very cool. 52
Waral waral	Caesitose perennial, seeds made into damper 8
Warnintji	Type of flying ant 26
Wartingkurra	No English equivalent 26
Wartunuma	Flying form of white ants
Warupunyu	Type of grass. Seeds ground to make damper 1, 10, 40
Watikutjarra	"Two men". Dreaming of two wise men travelling through area. Journey marked in actual physical landscape by two mesas together 103-5, 156, 185
Wayurta	Brush tail possum (lives in swamp) 8, 82
Wiitji	Military dragon lizard 136
Witjinpi	Fork-leafed corkwood. Uses: fire-saw and hearth; nectar obtained from flowers; burnt bark mixed with goanna fat applied to burns and skin complaints; necklaces made from round seeds
Witjirrki	Bush fig 70
Yanpakarratja	Non venomous snake 68
Yanpurrtju	Spinifex hopping mouse 70

Yinta	Waterhole in one's country 84, 145
Yipiri	Long stems from spinifex 80
Yirrakampa	Sugar bushtucker 68, 69
Yitakatji	Type of grass. Seeds collected from nest of particular ant, cleaned, ground into paste, made into bush damper 40, 57, 138
Yurrany	Rainy season, time of flying ants, sugar bushtucker 9, 21, 24

Reference:

Valiquette, Hilaire, 1993. *A Basic Kukatja to English Dictionary*, Luurnpa Catholic School, Wirrimanu (Balgo), Western Australia

Index of place names

Paintings Index

Artist	Painting titles, stories

Photographic Index

General index

Name Index